D0810158

EDUCATION II

EDUCATION II —
The Social Imperative

VASIL M. KERENSKY
and
ERNEST O. MELBY

PENDELL
PUBLISHING
COMPANY

211067

PENDELL
PUBLISHING
COMPANY

International Standard Book Number: 0-87812-013-0
Library of Congress Catalog Card Number: 74-156846

Copyrighted 1971 by
Pendell Publishing Company
Midland, Michigan

All Rights Reserved
Published 1971
Printed in the United States of America

To

Dedicated to the memory of Donald O. Tatroe whose life and professional leadership were devoted to the future of education and mankind.

CONTENTS

CONTENTS (Cont'd)

CONTENTS (Cont'd)

CONTENTS (Cont'd)

PREFACE

The nineteen sixties have been a period of "agonizing reappraisal" for American education. The stark realities of our failure with the children of the poor present a disturbing picture to a society which since the days of Thomas Jefferson has seen education as the very foundation of a free society and since Horace Mann has viewed universal schooling as a major element in the achievement of the American Dream. The schools have always had their critics but never before have their criticisms been supported by so much evidence and for the first time even sympathetic observers speak of the possible end of the American Dream.

The nineteen sixties were characterized by a series of paradoxes in education. No country in the history of the world has ever brought as large a proportion of its youth and adults into formal educational institutions nor kept the average person in school for so long a period. The growth in public schools and colleges has been phenomenal. Perhaps most significant of all the greatest American consensus is that whatever the problem, education in the final solution. This consensus seems to persist even though failure is admitted in the education of disadvantaged children and even though there is serious question concerning the adequacy of education provided children from middle class homes.

Why the crisis? Why the paradox? What accounts for the failure? Has the public simply not provided enough money? Are the poor uneducable? Is it simply that educational science has not provided the know-how? Has the teaching profession failed? The authors do not believe there are any simple answers nor any single panacea on the horizon. Money is not the basic problem. We have ample evidence that all of us are educable. Education today suffers far more from failure to use the knowledge we have than from a lack of knowledge. It is, in our view, unfair to lay the blame on the teachers, or the home. The basic fact is we have a new society, a new world and we still operate under old educational concepts. We are entering a new phase in the history of the human condition. The age of Mankind I is in its twilight and the dawn for Mankind II has had its beginning.

Tomorrow's society demands new qualities and characteristics. It is the learning man that will make possible the learning society. It is the understanding, compassionate man that can build the education-centered community that tomorrow demands. Relatively few understand Mankind II. Steps into the future are always uncertain. However, we know that only a very few do unskilled labor in the new society. All must have saleable skills in the new society. All must respect themselves. All must be able to relate creatively to their fellow men. All must feel responsible for the welfare of other men.

If the experiences of the nineteen sixties have proved anything about formal education they have forcibly indicated that the present system of education has become obsolete. The present establishment cannot produce men who can measure up to the problems and challenges presented by Mankind II. The present establishment when augmented and strengthened by various innovations does not do what needs to be done. What is it that needs to be done? Children from all economic backgrounds must be given an opportunity to learn. All children must learn. Failure cannot be countenanced.

From an international point of view, American education is distinguished and noted for a high degree of innovation. A high proportion of the innovations are good. Relevant and more practical curricula are desirable, yet the curriculum alterations of the present structure have not materially helped the disadvantaged to learn. Methodological changes under the present structure have not rescued the children of the poor. Team teaching, teaching machines, audio-visual aids, performance contracting, all have their good points but even when used to their fullest they have done little for the children of the poor who reside in the inner cities and other economically disadvantaged sections of America. Another decade or even a century of piecemeal innovation is not likely to solve the basic weaknesses that are apparent in the present educational system.

While the attention of the past decade has been sharply focused on the problems of educating the disadvantaged, educators and laymen alike are beginning to ask another question: Why do so many continue to be disadvantaged in so prosperous a society? They are asking not only: How do we educate the children of the ghetto, but why do we have the ghetto? To answer these questions calls for an examination of the entire educational system and its impact on all members of American society. When this is done it is necessary to face up to the reality that the present educational structure is not giving us the compassionate man, the learning man. It is not contributing as much as it should toward making our citizens both responsible and effective in creating a better society. It is the whole system that must be changed. For Mankind II we must create Education II; an education based on new assumptions, new goals, new programs and new attitudes on the part of both lay and professional participants.

The first assumption we must change is that some children will inevitably fail. The cliches run something like this. "School is not for them", or "Educate the best and sack the rest". The decision to educate only a proportion of American Youth becomes a self-fulfilling prophecy. We build failure into our educational programs. The new assumption must be: All children and all adults can learn and will learn if education creates a proper climate for learning. No single innovation, whether it be team teaching or the lighted schoolhouse can, by itself, create this climate. If the educator pins his faith on a single device or program he is doomed to failure. In a TV program entitled "A Day in the Life of America", a mother takes her child to the hospital emergency room where the girl is found to have a high temperature. The temperature persists and finally the child goes into convulsions. The concern of the medical team can be read in the faces of the group. The commentator then tells that "there are twelve hands on this child", six skilled medical personnel have pooled their resources in a desperate effort to save the child's life. Everything possible is being done. "All the stops are pulled." The important point is that there is a basic attitude that everything possible must be done. To do less would be to fail to meet one's professional and human obligation. The educational profession has rarely made such an assumption. It usually provides only the facilities on a mass basis but does not make sure that each child is given the help and attention he needs.

A second assumption that needs challenging and changing is that the schoolroom is the child's entire education. There has been much talk about educating the whole child, but practice has assumed that the schoolroom is the child's whole education. In reality it is the whole community that educates the child. It is the community that provides the climate for learning. Education must therefore concern itself with the whole community, seeking constantly to involve its resources and improve the whole environment. A true education-centered community is dynamic. It is in motion, and in continuous growth. Educational leaders should give priority, not to doing things for people, but to helping people to do things for themselves. This means risk-taking. Not all of what a community does and attempts to improve its life will be successful. The community must be given a chance to learn from its mistakes as well as from its successes.

A third assumption to be challenged is the archaic view that knowledge is the end of education, and that teaching is a scientific and technical endeavor. In accepting the above assumption, we have traditionally concluded that what the teacher knows is therefore more important than what the teacher is. Teaching is not *a* science. Teaching is an art, and in the arts the artist is the all important factor. This does not diminish the importance of knowledge, nor does it play down the role of science. The artistry of the teacher is manifested in his ability to utilize the increasingly large contributions made by the scientific community. As a creative artist, the teacher respects the child, has confidence in his learning capacity, is willing to join him in the learning experience and most importantly cares about the welfare of the child. In a word, compassion is the touchstone of the art of teaching.

Finally, present assumptions regarding the administration and control of education must be re-examined in the light of the needs of Education II. If the Individual children are to be free to learn, the teacher must be free to teach and the school must be free to perform its proper role in a community totally mobilized for education. Under the present centrally controlled bureaucratic organization, children are not free to learn, teachers are not free to teach, schools are not free to serve their communities and the people of the community have no effective way of either influencing the educational program or participating in its development. The development of an appropriate control system for education is one of the prime tasks for educational and community leaders in the decades ahead.

Education II addresses itself to the urgency for a new education operating under new assumptions. It treats briefly the social changes which have made existing education ineffective and obsolete. The experiences with present education have taught the educational profession a great deal. While no one can describe Education II in a definitive way, we have considered some of the major approaches which may be made in an effort to give all citizens a new and dynamic education.

The authors acknowledge their indebtedness to all their colleagues and students who have inspired most of the ideas presented. Special appreciation is extended to Mr. Frank J. Manley, Mr. C. S. Mott and the Mott Foundation for the creation of laboratories in which it has been possible to examine community challenges and appraise the functioning of existing educational programs. The experience of participating in the Mott Inter-University Clinical Preparation Program, now in its seventh year of operation and the association with the many brilliant men and women who served as interns in the project, the freedom given to faculty and students participating in the program all helped shape the thinking on which this volume is based.

The authors are especially indebted to their friend and colleague, Dr. J. D. Logsdon, Professor of Educational Administration at Florida Atlantic University for his most careful and helpful reading of the material and important editorial comments.

CHAPTER I

**THE CHALLENGE OF
THE URBAN COMMUNITY**

The Challenge
of the Urban Community

THE URBAN SCHOOL — Broken Dreams, Broken Lives

"The supreme question before mankind to which I shall not live to know the answer - is how men will be able to make themselves willing and able to save themselves."

Walter Lippman

Fifty years ago the educational wastelands were in the remote rural areas, a condition which the school consolidation movement sought to remedy and did to some degree. Today, the places in which education is failing most signally are to be found in the great cities, in slum areas, crowded with the culturally, economically and educationally disadvantaged.

The significance of our failure in urban areas becomes greater when we review our population trends. More than eighty-five per cent of the American people now live in 212 metropolitan areas which encompass eighty per cent of our productive industry. These areas will double in population within the next twenty-five years. The authors challenge any reasonable perceptive person to study first hand the social and educational problems of our great cities and come away without sleepless nights over the prospects for our country.

Statistics indicate the dimensions of the problems we face. Black people in our country have historically been deprived of educational and cultural opportunities, and so have Puerto Ricans, Mexicans and Appalachian whites.

When school opened in the fall of 1970 in Detroit, more than sixty per cent of the public school children were black. The percentage for St. Louis was over sixty-five; for Washington, D. C. the percentage was greater than ninety per cent.

To the burden of deprivation must be added the impact of poverty. Studies of school achievement indicate that there is a straight-line relationship between the income of the parents and the achievements of the children in school. The children of the poor tend to get the poorest and oldest school buildings and the least experienced teachers. This is not because school authorities plan it this way but because the culturally deprived crowd into the center of our cities where the buildings are old. Since most teachers are middle-class oriented people with middle class values, most try to avoid schools with children from the slums with the result that schools in slum areas get the teachers by assignment. Such teachers hope and try to be assigned to outlying areas as soon as they get a chance.

It would be a mistake to see the inner city problem as primarily involving black people. The inner city crisis is a problem of the poor. In New York, the poverty of the black is shared by that of the Puerto Ricans; in Phoenix, Arizona it is largely a problem involving Spanish Americans. It is the poor who populate the inner cities, and it is the poor with whom our schools are most ineffective.

While it is true that there are two poor whites for every poor black, the fact is that nearly half of all blacks fall into the prevailing poverty classification and it is well to note that etiology of black poverty differs significantly from that of white poverty.

Crime, prostitution and dope addiction flourish in the ghetto. In one city's low income black district, crimes against persons were thirty-five times as numerous as in a high income district. More than three-fourths of crimes committed by blacks are against other blacks.

In all of this—unemployment, crime, family break-up, health problems— the failure of our schools as the major social institution is a central cause. The black, the other minority groups, and the poor white are poor because they are unemployed or underemployed. They are unemployed because they are largely unemployable in the present labor market. They are unemployable because they lack a saleable skill and the unskilled jobs are growing scarcer. These jobs have been falling in proportion for many years.

4

A glance at the United States economy in 1930 will reveal that one in four of the American work force was engaged in unskilled labor. In 1970, only one in sixteen was so engaged. In 1930, only sixteen per cent of our work force was engaged in high level professions, technical and managerial work, while in 1970 this percentage was over thirty. This decade will mark the economic shift from a producing nation to one primarily concerned with providing services. During the 1950's the percentage of unemployed with less than a high school education increased while the unemployment percentages for those with a high school diploma decreased. The individual with high-level training had a better chance to get a job in 1970 than he had in 1950. During this same period, the beginning of a downward trend of opportunity for those without specialized skills became evident.

Education is an increasingly large factor in employment. The demand is for workers with skill and preparation. The employment patterns also take on racial and geographical overtones. For decades, blacks and Appalachian whites suffered social, economic and educational deprivation due to the lack of resources to prosper in a rural agrarian society, because of their tenant status. Today, they are tenants of the city, isolated in the ghetto, while resources for employment have shifted to locations that are inaccessible to low income groups.

A study of the relationship between education, job opportunities and employment indicates that a relevant education is the key to full employment. This may be a slight exaggeration but it is crystal clear that there are shortages in the professions and in managerial and highly technical pursuits. America needs twice as many doctors, twice as many effective teachers, four times as many dentists, four times as many nurses as we now have. They would closely approach the current number of unemployed.

Many are working at jobs beneath their levels of ability. This has a damaging effect upon them, and they fill vacancies that should be open to unemployed persons of lesser abilities. We need to see to it that each of us is prepared for the highest level job for which he is capable. This is one of education's very important responsibilities. Shortages are at the high levels of competence. This situation has an important bearing on college attendance. It is not enough to provide college education for the upper quarter, or the upper half of high school graduating classes. The upper two-thirds should have college opportunities. At present, only half of the upper third gets a college education. The failure of the other half to get the education they are capable of using in their own development is a tragic loss which our society can ill afford. Moreover, as teachers of these bright students in elementary and high schools, educators cannot escape responsibility for failure to show them the excitement in further education. Thus we see that the present educational structure is failing the poor, and this failure is one of the root causes of the crisis in the decaying cities.

If society needs a final blow to make us realize the magnitude of the problem we face, we can take a look to the future. In the next ten years, thirty million young people will be added to the work force. If current educational levels and accomplishments continue, seven and one-half million of these will be without a high school diploma and two and one-half million will not have finished the eighth grade. It is important that we recognize what faces us and undertake the task of preparing children and youth for our new automated society.

Teachers and others in education like to believe, indeed probably must believe, that education is the instrumentality by means of which our urban problems must ultimately be solved or kept under control. This is far from true for our existing urban schools.

THE BREAKDOWN OF URBAN LIFE

There is a new generation of immigrants in our cities. They are strangers in a strange land. They are strangers to urban living, to modern technology, and to the original inhabitants of our metropolitan areas.

The strangers constitute nearly half and in some cases more than half of our large city population. The strangers are usually black, they are generally poor, and they usually come from rural backgrounds. The Negro population in America is estimated at 21.4 million. Of these, 14.6 million live in cities, and the relationship between poverty and the Negro population is well-documented.

Our cities have become poor . . . poor . . . not broke! There is an important distinction here. Broke is to be temporarily without money, ideas or information. Poor is another phenomenon altogether. Poor is to be down, without money, ideas, information and without hope. The description of poverty and the poor not only describes many of the inhabitants of the American cities but also describes the general social and economic climate that permeates much of America's thinking with respect to the cities.

The American City has become a wasteland in many respects. The problems that confront our cities need little or no elaboration. America has abandoned her cities to the old, the poor, the black and the very young. Neglect of our cities has created problems which threaten our very existence. The American City is thus faced with a myriad of urgent and unattended social and economic problems. We are confronted with the problems of:

Crime
Pollution
Drug Abuse
Unemployment
Sub-standard Housing - Decaying Neighborhoods
High Dropout Rates - Low Achievement
Rising Welfare Costs
Alienation Between the Races

The American Cities are on the verge of self-strangulation in their own crime, pollution, transportation problems and most importantly in the apparent inability to cope with these and other problems. The urgency and seriousness of the problem is further illustrated by the fact that approximately eighty-five per cent of our population lives in or in close proximity to American Cities. We are no longer a rural America. However, much of our mentality, much of our frame of reference appears to be based on rural assumptions—assumptions that are no longer applicable for a mature, protean and rapidly changing society.

The phrase "inner city" has become synonymous with serious educational disorders and problems. A half century ago the rural areas were seen as the "educational wasteland", the areas which provided the least educational opportunity. In fifty years, the locus of the problem has moved from the rural areas to the center of the megalopolis. This transformation has come about as a result of one of the greatest migrations in American history. In 1910 ninety-one per cent of the nation's ten million Negroes lived in the rural South and only twenty-seven per cent lived in the cities. By 1970 the Negro population had more than doubled and the rural, urban pattern has nearly reversed itself. Black America is now found in urban America and the migration continues.

Compounding the problem is the fact that unemployment and underemployment for much of the black population is a constant specter. In some low income, black neighborhoods, unemployment and underemployment constitutes thirty-three per cent for blacks between eighteen and twenty-five years of age. This is a figure nearly nine times as high as the overall rate for the nation and twice as high as figures that represented the "Great Depression".

While in this chapter we are primarily concerned with the urban challenge to the field of education, it should be pointed out that the urban centers at the present moment challenge the very stability of our society. There are those who believe that a city like New York has become ungovernable and that our whole system of government which had its beginnings in a fairly rural type of society is facing insurmountable difficulties in adapting itself to the control of our urban concentrations. The impact of the large city on the life, the character, attitude and behavior of people is a vast subject for which adequate treatment cannot be provided at this point. The total problem, however, has enormous significance for education. Urban life urgently calls for changed attitudes on the part of people. Among urban dwellers there is a great sense of loss of community, a growing sense of anonymity and lack of a feeling of responsibility for others. The very fact that one is in daily contact with large masses of people, to whom he has no particular relationship, causes the individual to look upon people, in the mass at least, as objects and things rather than as human beings. Much publicity has been given to those instances in which individuals have witnessed attacks and killings but refrained from coming to help because of the feeling of not wanting to be involved. It would have been unthinkable for a farmer in a rural area to refuse to help his neighbor because of fear of involvement. In fact, a feeling of involvement with ones neighbors was a basic fact of rural life.

The widespread escape on the part of well-to-do dwellers to the suburbs and again to further removed areas is an example of our inability to cope with our responsibilities. When we find the situation uncomfortable, we seek escape rather than to remain and solve the problem. When our middle class professional and managerial groups in society leave the city to reside in the suburbs they not only remove themselves and their families but to a large extent they remove their interests and their contributions to the improvement of city life. The human ingredients necessary to isolate, analyze and remedy the problems have escaped to the suburbs.

Not only are the big cities now the wasteland area of education but they are the areas that have the lowest financial resources. The center of affluence has moved from the large cities to the suburban areas. As an example, in thirty-seven of the largest United States metropolitan areas the average per capita expenditure for education in these central cities is $82.00. The corresponding expenditure in the suburbs is $113.00. Making the comparison on a per student basis the comparable figures are $449.00 for cities and $575.00 for the suburbs.[1] Moreover, the indications are that with the passing of the years the comparisons will more strongly favor the suburbs since much of the industry providing a tax base in cities is also moving out from the center of the city to the suburban areas thus impoverishing the city at the center and enriching the outlying areas. Tax evaluation in our leading cities has been on the decline since 1947, and the end is not in sight. Thus, the picture confronting educational leaders in our cities is less revenue and an increased burden of the number of children to be educated.

Generally, the public does not realize that living in the large city is an expensive way of life. It is not only that the city expenditures for education and valuations for taxation are dropping, the complicating factor is that non-educational expenditures constitute sixty-eight per cent of total public expenditures whereas in the suburbs they constitute approximately forty-seven per cent. Schools are competing with other city agencies for the public dollar and by comparison the schools are suffering.

The extreme difficulties confronting cities in financing all public services have long been known. One effort has been to ask the legislature for help. Generally speaking, not much help has been forthcoming. One of the reasons is that a large proportion of the legislatures is rural minded and has scant sympathy with the cities and their problems. Compounding the problem is the rising cost of services, the inflationary spiral and a "taxpayer revolt" that manifests itself in vetoes of local tax requests.

The Impact of Rapid Change

The most perplexing task facing education in today's world is that of trying to cope with the issue of change. Discussions concerning the tempo of change run the risk of becoming a tiring concept and a cliche. For many years it was popular to suggest that the only thing constant was change. This is no longer true. New terms and concepts are necessary to understand and describe the changes we are experiencing. Change at one time could be described in linear terms; in fact, we lived in a nascent, predictable and somewhat controllable world. Today change has taken on entirely new dimensions. It is protean, explosive, accelerated, and unpredictable. The rate of change

---

[1] Alan K. Campbell, "Inequities of School Finance," *Saturday Review*, Jan. 11, 1969, pp. 44-48.

is accelerating. Knowledge may be doubling in ten year cycles. We will no longer make reference to history in terms of centuries, but in terms of decades.

Change has become so intensified that efforts to understand its implications are difficult, and it is even more difficult to control or direct it. Margaret Mead holds that the impact of change has made the parents of teenagers immigrants to the society in which they live. What Mead is suggesting is that many native born Americans have become immigrants to the society in which they live by virtue of the speed of change that characterizes life in a modern, technological, pre-figurative society.

Many of our problems in society in general and education in particular, stem from a tendency to think in terms of a non-existent world. Much of our thinking and planning has been based on assumptions that if once true are no longer valid. It is difficult for many of us to comprehend that the year 2000 A.D. is closer in time than 1932. Yet, much of our thinking on educational decision-making and the establishment of priorities is more closely related to the past than the future. Paraphrasing General Motor's Charles Kettering, if automobile designers built cars with the same perspective that characterizes much of educational planning they would put seats in automobiles that faced the rear. Marshall McLuhan suggests that we are heading into the future with our eyes fixed firmly on the rear view mirror.

There are other implications for education as a result of the accelerating rate of change. One of these is the historical principle of "limitation of choice". The principle suggests that when persons, groups or institutions wait to attack a problem the delay decreases the number of alternatives. In a world that moved slowly and in a more predictable manner there was time for quiet deliberation and the temporary neglect of pressing problems was not too serious. In today's world, productive alternatives may disappear overnight.

Missing Sense of Community

In addition to the impact of change, much of American life is experiencing a "missing sense of community". America has become an urban society. New communities spring up overnight. Eighty-five per cent of our population lives in 212 urban areas that comprise approximately three per cent of the land area. We have witnessed a great migration in the last thirty years and many Americans have not come to grips with its full impact. Urbanization has brought us closer together physically thus creating many new contractual and compulsory relationships. A real dichotomy exists. We live closer together, but we don't know each other. We often execute or contract from the confines of our automobiles. We eat in the car and are entertained in the isolation of our cars. In Los Angeles and other metropolitan areas, we can even pay our last respects to a deceased friend at a drive-in funeral home.

Living close together doesn't necessarily create a community. Urban America has become self-oriented, diffused, molecular, and neutral to the needs of the molar community. Durkheim defines this development as an "organically solitary society": - where society is held together by the interdependence of its parts. The division of labor is a result of a struggle for existence, and the specialization of labor stimulates individualism and differentiation. People are heterogeneous and their mental and moral similarities disappear. Young people refer to this phenomena as: "Doing your own thing". The result has been the loss of a "collective conscience", or sense of community.

Self and society (community) are "twin born". A loss of this needed perspective or equilibrium between self and community characterizes Urban America. The American housing subdivision and suburban housing developments characterize and illustrate the paradox of close geographical proximity and remote affective and collective community involvement. The same is true in the crowded cities. The American ghetto closely resembles a frontier settlement during a Gold Rush inhabited with self-seekers and individuals struggling to survive. The similarities that exist in the decline of a "sense of community" in inner city settings and the Boom Town Gold Rush settlements are well established historical patterns.

One illustration of the missing sense of community and the lack of perspective between the needs of self and the needs of the community can be dramatized if the reader steps out in his backyard and visualizes hitting eight-iron golf shots in several different directions. The premise here is that even the poorest golfer can drop golf balls into the yards of neighbors whom he does not know! For apartment dwellers, the situation is even more dramatic. One may stand face to face at the washstand, separated from neighbors you do not know by only a medicine cabinet. Gillette! Gesellschaft![2]

[2] Ferdinand Tonnies analysis of the dynamics of a societal continuum between a Gemeindschaft and Gesellschaft is very relevant to a consideration of the phenomenon of a "missing sense of community". Robert Redfield has formulated a folk-urban typology that has implications for the new world confronting most Americans.

11

It is not possible to reclaim the past and the former "sense of community". If we could, it is questionable that most Americans would want to reclaim the "good ole days". But, our very survival as a nation depends upon new approaches to establishing a "new sense of community".

Too many of our citizens are unable to comprehend the disappearance of the rural community and the emergence of an urban society. The most casual review of census statistics regarding urban America in the light of current practices is alarming. As an illustration, John Lindsay, Mayor of New York City, is a frequent guest on late evening television shows. During the summer months he made a special appearance to invite concerned citizens of the city to make donations for street basketball goals, portable swimming pools and funds to open store front recreation centers. He asked for these donations in the name of the city's children who are out of school for the summer. Why are schools closed during the summer months? Why are children out of school for two and a half to three months from early June to mid-September? Schools are closed under the false assumption that our children and young adults are out harvesting crops! They are not harvesting crops! Many are out harvesting our cities!

Unnecessary Duplication of Services

Closely related to the inability to effectively mobilize the human and physical resources of our highly complex, organizational society is the tendency toward an unnecessary duplication of services. The inability or unwillingness to cooperate or coordinate creates a montage of duplication, an overlapping that saps the spiritual and financial strength of most communities.

Communities are asked to support with tax dollars: school plants, and sites, multi-million dollar plants that are on five to twenty acre sites. These facilities often lie idle after 3:30 p.m. and for two and a half months during the summer.

Yet, the same taxpayer is asked to support the purchase of a park and recreational site of five to twenty acres to be used primarily after school hours, weekends and the summer months.

This is compounded by a request for a multi-million dollar "Community Center" with a community swimming pool and community auditorium. Again, the prime use is for after school and evenings. Two blocks away may be found an empty high school, a closed swimming pool and an empty auditorium.

Next, a neighborhood youth center is opened with federal dollars in an old store front, at exorbitant rent, across from a school. The Center is often staffed and attended by the same people as the neighborhood school. The only difference is a separate administrative staff and separate overhead costs.

Communities build a vocational education center for job retraining. Clients usually attend evening classes. The facilities, since they are financed by the federal government, are usually imposing. One mile away an antique high school shop is dark in the evenings and during the day the staff struggles with the potential dropouts training on obsolete machinery, assuring the vocational job training center its future clients.

These are only a few illustrations of the waste and unnecessary duplications that deprive children and adults of educational, social, cultural and recreational services. The unnecessary duplication is also using precious dollars that could be reallocated and redirected toward the myriad of problems that face each community.

Failure to Mobilize Human and Physical Resources

Another baffling problem that faces both society in general and education in particular is our apparent inability to mobilize existing resources for an attack on economic and social problems.

Educators, business and industrial leaders have for years decried the needless waste of sixty to one hundred billion dollars worth of tax-supported school buildings standing idle in the late afternoon, early evening, every Saturday and Sunday, and for the most part three entire months during the summer.

Utilization of school buildings in terms of 7:00 a.m. to 10:00 p.m., six days a week, and fifty-two weeks a year, amounts to over 4,700 usable hours per year. The typical public school plant is used less than one-fourth of this time. This is inconceivable waste! If the automobile industry used its capital outlay to this extent, an economical car would in all probability cost the consumer in excess of $12,000. In our day and age, it is not only a waste of a valuable resource, it is a tragedy in this time of critical and crucial need for education and training.

Equally devastating is the waste of a tremendous resource of brilliant creative people in every community. Individuals with unique talents, skills,

13

hobbies, interests, and untapped talents are left out because they are "not certified". This is tragic!

At the core of many of our social and economical problems is our seeming inability to mobilize, coordinate and fully utilize the tremendous resources that are available.

The reasons of our failure are generally found in the minds of men, rather than constraints of facilities, finances or human potential. Cities are decaying, human needs go unmet, children fail to reach their full potential while:

— Organizations fail to assess and reassess their raison d'etre.

— Organizational leaders jealously guard their own spheres of influence, functions and facilities.

— Organizational effectiveness is measured on outdated or false assumptions.

— Individual self-interest - Organizational self-interest is self serving. Organizational status supersedes the institutional or organizational goals. Illustration: A well-dressed official pulled up in his Cadillac and announced that he is in the "War on Poverty", while one astute observer announced that "It looks like you've won"!

— Organizational patterns and attitudes develop that exhibit unwillingness to share success and have even a greater unwillingness to admit mistakes.

One may conclude that the taxpayer revolt is in part a veto of requests for additional funds to support social services and educational programs that fail to totally mobilize and utilize existing resources.

Bureaucracy

One of the most difficult and baffling problems our society and public education faces is the stifling effect of tall, unresponsive bureaucracies. Attacks on bureaucracy, like attacks on sin, are very popular. Bureaucracy and large organizational abuses are everybody's whipping boy. Robert Townsend's *Up the Organization*,[3] "How to Stop the Corporation from

---

[3] Robert Townsend, *Up the Organization*, "How to Stop the Corporation from Stifling People and Strangling Profits." New York: Alfred A. Knopf, 1970.

Stifling People and Strangling Profits" has captured the fancy of many readers. Townsend's concerns are as appropriate for the educational structure as they are for business. Our large, tall, hierarchial organizational patterns are literally strangling our schools and the people in them.

We must find ways to free school and individual teachers to be different, to depart, to explore, and to be unique in serving the individual and communities they serve. Too often the reverse has been true. The educational organization copying many standardization procedures that have long ago been abandoned by business and industry has moved the decision-making process further away from the operational level, the classroom. Effective organizations strive for the reverse and have moved the decision-making process as close to the operating level as possible. However, the administrative pattern in education has been that of providing solutions from the Central Office.

The effect of over-standardization and pyramidal organizational patterns have been disastrous. Not only is it an ineffective organizational pattern for problem solving, it has become a major problem in itself. Pogo says: "I have discovered the enemy - it is us"!

How does the tall, inflexible organization shatter initiative, imagination, creativity? Just a few of the abuses that stifle the education process are:

- Requisitions with three to ten copies that must be approved by all the people on the way to the District or Central Office.

- An attitude that if the forms are right - everything is right.

- Three weeks to receive a film.

- Requisitions to the Central Office to get a school toilet repaired or a window fixed.

- A full semester to get delivery on a $10.00 item.

- Central Office approval for school-community correspondence.

- Specialist in everything!
    Community Relations
    Media
    Public Relations
    Curriculum
    Personnel

15

The result - "That is not in my area!" . . . "Call on the Specialist!"

- Central Office and District Staff whose major effort often revolve around sending memos to each other, and keeping their secretaries busy.

  A common feeling in the Washington Pentagon, is jocularly, to the effect that each employee has one aim, namely, that every item arriving on his desk during the day must be on some other desk by the next day.

- Budget prepared at the Central Office level, often with little or no input from local schools. The result - feast in some areas, famine in others!

- Status panic among educational personnel. Egg walkers who are more concerned about organizational protocol than the education of children.

- Elaborate organizational charts that have little meaning to anyone, especially the teachers, the children and the community.

- Computer Specialists that often tell you what can't be done because the computer is not programmed for it, or

- Automation of things that don't matter, false, superficial efficiencies that have little human or educational meaning.

- Expensive and time-consuming staff meetings, search for: "Are we all together on this solution?"

- *Reaction* at top echelon levels rather than *action* at the operational level.

- Expensive policy manual that emphasizes "what can't be done".

- Central hiring procedures. Many building principals meet their new staff members for the first time at a preschool conference.

- Duplication of services and demands for form reports to satisfy the ego needs of various sub-systems.

- Standardized luncheon menus.

- Standardized textbooks.

- Central personnel offices reshuffling inept teachers from one school to another.
- Closets full of orange construction paper and not a sheet of black paper in the school and Halloween a week away.

The list is endless, the red tape staggering. The suggestion here is not anti-organizational. It is not an appeal for chaos or entropy. The problem stems from over-organization. Artificial, self-seeking, counter-productive organizational, bureaucratic patterns that sap individual and group energies. The large, remote educational structure has become dysfunctional. Centralization had depersonalized and dehumanized education to the point that the educational, organizational structure is one of American education's biggest problems:

Every new opinion, at its starting is precisely in the minority of one.

    Thomas Carlyle
    Great Ideas of Western Man

Decentralization is not fragmentation.

It is a system that can give cohesive strength to its individual parts.

As a corporate opinion, it is based on a sense of freedom and the result is communication with people in a framework that is easier to handle and more meaningful in relation to their specific problems.

The corporation itself may grow and become somewhat impersonal by size itself. But the problems of the people it is in existence for, remain personal in size.

A system of decentralization then is a way to continue conversation.

PARADOXES OF OUR TIME

"We know that happiness is more than material well-being, that conscience is more than simple fear, that love is more than sex, that moral authority is more than political power, and that community is more than organization."
                        Kingman Brewster, Jr.

17

America is in the midst of the greatest prosperity the nation has ever known. We have widespread affluence and at least two-thirds of our people enjoy a level of comfortable living which can be called middle class in the economic sense. This is proportionately the largest middle class in history. Great changes are taking place in working conditions, in labor relations, race relations and in the availability of education. Progress in these areas is more rapid than at any previous time in our history. Yet we face unprecedented social unrest, increasing incidents of crime, violent protest, not only by black poor but by university students. There is a growing movement for separatism on the part of black people at a time when the status of black people in our society is improving at a more rapid rate than ever before in history.

To many, the greatest paradox of all is that our quantitative gains in education and our spreading prosperity have not brought us individual happiness, domestic peace or international understanding. Perhaps Emerson had the explanation when he said "Things are in the saddle and riding mankind". President Nixon pointed to the same diagnosis when he said: "We are rich in things but ragged in spirit." Many young people agree by criticizing our present concepts of success such as making money and attaining power. There are paradoxes all around us causing consternation, bewilderment, confusion and immobility.

We are experiencing the greatest prosperity a nation has ever known, yet our wealth is not generally accompanied by happiness. Our young people are turning their backs on middle class values and too often their search for new meaning is in vain, resulting in an escape from reality in drugs.

We are building new communities at an unprecedented rate. Yet our citizens can't find a community. We simply move closer together physically while widening the emotional gulf that prevents a true sense of community. The paradox of physical proximity and emotional remoteness is all around us. Mass media have made it possible to instantaneously become aware of problems and successes from around the world. But the death two doors down the street, the birth on the next block, the problems of the "boy next door" go unnoticed in the impersonal society that characterizes urban life.

We are experiencing an unprecedented degree of non-conformity, but the non-conformity manifests itself in new conformities. The dress codes, hair styles and drug abuse provide avenues for new types of conformity by many youth. The cocktail circuit, noisy small talk, worship of materialistic things characterize the conformity of the "over thirty" generation. The new conformity is characterized by an attitude of "do your own thing", even if it is in mud that is knee deep, because peer expectations require it. In other words, doing one's thing really means doing the group thing.

There is also the paradox of a movement toward secularism accompanied by the rise of a myriad of psuedo religions, cults and a search for deeper spiritual meaning.

The striking forms of paradox in various aspects of American life detract from social progress. The widespread prosperity tends to blind people to the areas of poverty and injustice. There is also a tendency to dwell on the American economic success with a feeling that, if only twenty per cent are poor, the problem cannot be too important. Such complacency is based on a very inaccurate reading of the social signs of our times. All over the world, the mood of poor people and the oppressed has gone through a marked change. They now know they are miserable. They also know that the large middle classes do not suffer the same misery. They want what comfortable people have and they aim to get it by one means or another. It is therefore doubtful whether any society can remain stable if it has a substantial minority of its people in poverty and suffering from discrimination.

THE CHALLENGE TO EDUCATION

No perceptive educator in America today can go about his work without being reminded daily that his country and his world are in crisis. The distant din of the Vietnam War, the crisis in the Middle East, the "war" of recent summers in our cities here at home, the unrest on our college campuses, the seeming paralysis of the war on poverty, the mounting data on crime and lawlessness, the ugly backlash against democratic institutions in many areas — all these are elements in the crisis.

But these are only the symptoms of our confusion as a people. As a nation we are sharply divided. Basically, we are passing through a crisis in will power, the will to do what we know is right, what can be expected of us in terms of our traditions of freedom and human rights.

Thus, when the educator looks out the school window today, what he sees is a country divided, frustrated, and losing confidence in itself and its leaders. The teaching profession believes that education can help America to meet this crisis. The rest of society aids and abets the teacher in this belief, for perhaps the greatest consensus in America today is to the effect that whatever serious problems we face, education is the ultimate solution. How soundly based is this consensus? Will our present education save us if only we spend enough money on it? Will it give us the will to bring "liberty and justice to all?"

As educators we cannot escape responsibility for the crisis, nor can we avoid a careful examination of our present education in the light of the challenges of our technological, highly urbanized society.

Readers of the Chicago Tribune were recently greeted by the headlines: "Study Rips Chicago's Schools." A sub-heading continues: "School System Near Collapse."[4] The article that follows suggests that Chicago schools are falling of their own dead weight. The Tribune goes on to say that if education is a *battle* against the ignorance and the multitude of social and economic problems that ignorance produces, the Chicago School Board has surrendered. The above story is not unique to Chicago. The feeling of frustration and desperation depicted in the above article are reoccurring all too often across America, in our large urban areas.

The pessimistic analysis described here may be too dismal as we enter the nineteen seventies. However, the most casual observer of the educational scene sees that education must undergo many dramatic changes if it is to respond to the demands of society between now and the millennium.

As the nineteen seventies begin, the authors might have addressed themselves to a review of educational and societal triumphs of the past several decades. Stories of success abound. However, we are approaching the next thirty years with a myriad of problems that need both short and long range attention. To avoid an assessment of problems that tear at the very fabric of our society would be both foolish and naive.

Mitchell Gordon in his volume *Sick Cities* makes the following statement:

> *Indeed the modern urban school is more likely to serve as a pressure cooker for differences, resentments, rivalries and intolerance than as an instrument capable of the greatest achievement of education, the sowing of respect for others, regardless of creed or color. The penalties for this failure may be exacted from society in many ways, through the aggravation of police problems, the erosion of national loyalties, the diminution of stimuli that are otherwise found in the questioning of prevailing patterns of life and thought and in the waste of human resources that results from too narrow an appreciation of individual worth.* [5]

[4] *Chicago Tribune*, Monday, June 8, 1970, p. 1.

[5] Mitchell Gordon, *Sick Cities*, New York: The MacMillan Company, p. 231.

Rather slowly but surely, even educators have been forced to reach the conclusion that our present educational system is a stark failure with the poor, with the inner city and with the black people and other minority groups. An even darker cloud is on the horizon, and that is the growing realization that in large measure the whole system is obsolete. We have been so enthralled by our problems with the disadvantaged that we have failed to see our larger failure with all children and all people. It is, of course, urgent that we be concerned with our inner cities and about race prejudice. But we are beginning to ask other questions. Why is it, that in the most highly developed nation in history, our affluent people both black and white tolerate slums? Why is it that white people generally fail to see what it means to be black in America? Why do many refuse to give equality and full citizenship to minority groups? Why have we so little perception of injustice. Why have we so little compassion?

Had education provided our citizens with compassion, a sense of oneness, and a responsibility for one's fellowman, the problem that now gives us an unsolved crisis might have been avoided. The fact is that our failure with the middle class is more basic than our failure with the poor. There is substance in the contention that our educational system extending from the first grade to graduate school may well be obsolete in today's society.

The large city has in effect thrown down the gauntlet, not only to our schools but also to all our social, economic and political institutions. It is in the megalopolis that all the agencies of government are threatened with near collapse. This is true whether the problem is pollution, crime, health or education. The city magnifies and intensifies every problem. Here are concentrated, the poor, the black, the disadvantaged of every description. But in no case are the resulting problems more complex or is the need for solution greater than in the area of education.

CHAPTER II

**INADEQUACY
OF
SCHOOLHOUSE EDUCATION**

Inadequacy of
Schoolhouse Education

INTRODUCTION

> *There was a child went forth everyday,*
> *And the first object he looked upon, that object he became,*
> *And that object became part of him for the day or a certain*
> *   part of the day,*
> *Or for many years or stretching cycles of years.*
> *The early lilacs became part of this child*
> *And the grass and white and red morning glories, and white*
> *   and red clover, and the song of the phoebe-bird,*
> *And the third month lambs and the sows pink-faint litter,*
> *   and the mare's foal and the cow's calf,*
> *And the noisy brood of the barnyard or by the mire of the*
> *   pond-side,* [1]

Walt Whitman

Even Walt Whitman sensed the true way in which education takes place. Since this time, countless teachers and students of education have pointed out that the child is educated by his whole life. Since this is true, schoolhouse education can never be more than a part of the child's educational experience.

[1]   Walt Whitman, Leaves of Grass, p. 293.

Yet schools have been very slow to act upon our outmoded belief. We have talked about educating the whole child and drifted into practices which seem to assume that we in the school are the child's whole education. Our experience with the disadvantaged has pulled us up short. Educators have had to face stark failure in an attempt to provide the whole child's education when the child, the parents and the community are all disadvantaged. In the process, we have been compelled to admit that schoolhouse education is inadequate and obsolete.

THE EDUCATIONAL PROGRAM IS OBSOLETE

It is . . . impossible to teach children in masses . . . A "class" is an arbitrary grouping of seemingly homogeneous beings, no two . . . anymore alike than two snowflakes. If it were possible to place children under a microscope, one would find the least of them inspiringly beautiful, distinctively designed. When we gather too many, flakes or children, the loveliness of individuality is lost and what we get is all white, the ultimate in neutrality.

Sam Levenson

As educators, we have an ambivalent attitude toward the school as an institution. We extol its merits and its role in society, yet in our hearts, if not in our minds, we know its weaknesses. Teachers work hard with children too often with a sad sense of failure. The public wonders about the wisdom of growing expenditures for education when crime steadily increases and large numbers of those who have been to school are functionally illiterate and without a saleable skill. We struggle to teach a child successfully, then discover that what we have tried so hard to accomplish has been destroyed by his experiences on the street and in the home. Even though we know that it is the child's whole environment that educates, that education takes place as a result of the interaction between the individual and the totality of his environment — we still keep trying to make the school the complete educational instrument. We continue to claim too much for what we can do in the school building from nine o'clock in the morning to three o'clock in the afternoon. It is not only in the ghetto that we fail. American children not served by our educational establishment are really everywhere. To use Peter Schragg's language:

> *They exist everywhere, but convention has almost wiped them from sight. They are not supposed to be there, are not perhaps supposed to believe even in their own existence. Thus, they function not for themselves but to define and affirm the position of others: those who are very poor or those who are affluent, those who go to college. In visiting the*

schools that they attend one must constantly define them, not by what they are but by what they are not and sometimes in talking to teachers and administrators one begins to doubt whether they exist at all.[2]

The evidence is all about us: blasted hopes, the dulled ambitions, the general tendency to settle for what is around the corner rather than for ultimate achievement. Disappointment and lower expectations slow the tempo of family life, lower the ambition of mothers and fathers, and contribute to cynicism on the part of community leaders.

The question is why all this sadness and disappointment? How does it happen? Again to use Schragg's language:

The instrument of oppression is the book. It is still the embodiment of the great mystery, learn to understand its secrets and great things will follow. Submit to your instinctive and natural boredom (lacking either the skills to play the game or the security to revolt), and we will use it to persuade you of your benighted incompetence.[3]

Schragg has told the story well. It does not sound good to us as teachers but it is the truth. The school is the final destructive force in the life of many children. In a society in which education is essential for decent survival, any educational system that is destructive must go. It is obsolete, it must be replaced.

Even if our present schools did well by all children, even if they did well by the poor and the black, even if they functioned effectively in our large cities and in the remote rural areas, the system is still obsolete. It will not do today to educate children with the idea that the education they receive in childhood and youth will last them for the remainder of their lives. It will not do to educate the children without educating the adults. It will not even be enough to educate children and the adults unless the quality of the education is such that a sense of social responsibility is developed on the part of the individual human being. Beyond his own sense of responsibility, the individual should acquire the practice of participating in the improvement of his own community. He can begin this in childhood and youth, and he can continue it throughout the length of his life. As he does continue it throughout the length of his life he can contribute to the education and the improvement of life for his fellow-

---

[2] Peter Schragg, "Growing Up on Mechanic Street", *Saturday Review*, March 21, 1970, p. 60.

[3] *Ibid*, p. 61.

man. In other words, we need an entirely different concept of education than the one that has characterized the American educational establishment thus far in our history. We need community schools, schools that are open whenever there are people who can profit from their programs. But community schools are not enough, unless the total educational program mobilizes all the resources of the community. It is not enough to inform people, to give them information and skills. We must also develop attitudes which are basic to the success of our free institutions.

Present education fails in nearly all of these particulars. It makes fallacious assumptions about the potential of human beings, holding that a significant proportion of the children are practically ineducable. It continues lock-step methods which assume that the growth patterns for all children are approximately the same. It lays the blame for the child's failure to achieve on the child himself and the background from which he comes. It dodges the responsibility of creating for each individual the kind of environment in which he can grow. It sees the problem of equality of opportunity in terms of equality of input when true equality will come about only when equality is measured in terms of output. It assumes that only teachers with certificates can teach, when we know that paraprofessionals, teacher aides, and lay people of many types of experience can be extremely useful in many instructional areas. In some areas, they are more effective than the professionals. Our present educational programs have too great an obsession with cognitive learning. They downgrade personality development as well as many areas in arts, literature and music. Too much of our education occurs in isolation, too little in the realities of everyday living.

No matter how difficult the educational challenge that confronts our country, no matter how expensive it may be in money and time-consuming in human effort, no matter the extent of the dedication required on the part of teachers, our free institutions will not survive unless education plays a more effective role than it is playing at the present moment. A new education, Education II, must be produced, a wholly new concept of adequacy, a new marshalling of resources, a new level of participation on the part of all of our people. An education must and can be built that will make the difference between success and failure for the American Dream.

The School's Scrap Heap

Among other shortcomings there are two basic characteristics of school-house education that contribute to its inadequacy. First in the work of the school, the child is daily confronted with demands he cannot meet, demands which the teacher and the administrator know he cannot meet. Since many children are seldom asked to do anything they are currently able to do, they are perforce educated in *failure*. This rank injustice is a built-in characteristic of the educational establishment. Cognitive learning is the school's major goal. Not only that, this cognitive learning must come at a specified chronological age regardless of the quality of the child's life before and after school entrance. The establishment operates this way even though it has impressive evidence that thousands of children are being destroyed each year. It does not seem to impress many teachers that studies in human development show widely variable growth curves. We know that children do not walk at the same age or talk at the same age. For some mysterious reason, we expect all children to read at six. When a child comes from a deprived home and community setting, he has a double disadvantage. The school expects him to do what he is not ready to do and marks him down when he fails, thus demonstrating to him that he cannot learn. In middle class homes and communities the same thing happens, though less frequently, but here the good home and other community influences repair some of the damage done by the school. Even where special programs of compensatory education are conducted, often little is done to educate the parents or to help them improve the community. Consequently, the work done by the school is often negated by outside influences.

The second characteristic of schoolhouse education which renders it ineffective in our current society is its failure to educate all the people of the community. It is more than an inadvertent failure. In many instances it is a studied effort to avoid dealing with parents and adults generally. No one can deny the teacher's reluctance to face parents. "If only they would let us alone," has too often been the attitude. Now the evidence concerning the power of the child's total environment is so convincing that schools are forced to consider parent and community attitudes. Often, however, the efforts made are examples of one-way communication rather than the development of a cooperative venture. Even though our best psychological evidence indicates that education takes place as a result of the interaction between the individual and the totality of his environment, we still keep trying to make the school the complete educational instrument. We subscribe to the concept that educating the whole child is a desirable one then delude ourselves into believing that this can take place within the confines of the schoolhouse.

Educators have traditionally turned to parents and citizens in the community, with reluctance and with no small amount of fear. We recall with dismay the days when lay people controlled education, visited schools to appraise their effectiveness, and we recall that it introduced lay ignorance

into the control of the schools. Current demands for more community participation in education bring back the ghosts of these earlier days.

The Closed Corporation

Academic people also suffer from an obsession with the power of knowledge. Academicians seem to take it for granted that a man who knows
what is right will do what is right, that the mastery of bodies of subject
matter somehow changes the behavior of people even though the persons
taught have had no opportunity to practice the principles involved. If children
show little interest in these organized bodies of subject matter, we blame
them for stupidity or banality and feel that in teaching the time-honored
materials, we are "throwing pearls before swine". Other teachers blame the
home and the community, saying "what can you expect of a boy who comes
from this kind of background?"

How often have you heard a teacher comment, "I can't do a thing for him,
the situation at home is impossible" . . . . *that* child from *that* family", or
" . . . . from *that* part of town". It is frustrating for teachers to know that
everything that might be accomplished during the school day may be undone
by the time the child walks by the corner drugstore. Many of our teachers
work in settings that are viewed as hopeless . . . the neighborhood is declining . . . the peer relationships are bad . . . parents don't care . . . family
situations are impossible. Teachers lament, "The only parents we see are the
parents of good students and we only see them at P.T.A. and even here
there is seldom any real communication".

These feelings of frustration exist to some degree in all of our schools,
but they are intensified in schools that serve socio-economically disadvantaged
areas.

To a degree, those who blame the home and the community are right.
What these teachers are really admitting is that present schools need support
in the form of good homes, good communities and good voluntary associations.
Our present schools work reasonably well in the middle class areas. In fact,
it appears that middle class children succeed academically in all kinds of
schools both good and poor. That is, they get passing marks, graduate, get
into college and become members of the middle class community. We do
not bother to ask about the extent to which these children have developed
their true potential, what they could have done had their abilities been
fully developed.

Educators and the public as well are led into fallacious thinking about education by the easy assumption that satisfactory marks and graduation are proof of the effectiveness of the schools as educational agencies. When the children come from the homes of the poor, the slum, the inner city or the remote rural areas . . . a near complete breakdown in educational effectiveness occurs. The present educational system's failure to meet the needs of large segments of our student population will continue until educators and community leaders reassess our assumptions regarding the type of education that can make a difference.

SCHOOL IS DULL AND IT'S EXCITING OUTSIDE

The changes that have taken place in life in the last century have added in geometric ratio to the excitement of life. An exploding technology has created a veritable wonderland of things and activities to fascinate children and youth. Think of the automobile and the many dimensions it has added to life; the wonder of space, the awesome nuclear bombs, the miracles of surgery and chemistry! A century ago there was more excitement within the books in a rural school library than in all of life outside as seen by the typical child. Today the reverse is the case. A very dull school is competing with a very exciting world outside. In fact, the contrast makes the school appear more dull than it actually is. Charles Silberman, in the process of conducting a study of education sponsored by the Carnegie Corporation, is quoted as saying:

> *The way the public schools are organized destroys spontaneity, initiative, and love of learning among the teachers as well as among the students. The public schools are quite literally destructive of human beings. I think they are the most grim joyless places on the face of the earth. They are needlessly authoritarian and repressive - not because teachers and principals are stupid or venal but because nobody ever asks why: why the rules or why the curriculum . . . and if our concern is with education we cannot restrict our attention to the schools for education is not synonymous with schooling, and teachers are not the only educators.*[4]

The typical educator's response to all this really misses the point. The remedies we propose are inside the schoolhouse, the new mathematics, the new science, the new English, team teaching, teaching machines and the

---

[4]   Charles E. Silberman, "Crisis in the Classroom", *New York: Random House,* 1970.

like. Why not try using the exciting world outside? Why not let the primary actors in this exciting world help with the teaching? Why not let the banker help us understand a bank? Why not let the mayor of the city or other city official help us understand city government? Why insulate the children away from what they study?

"Speaking of English informal schools, Silberman says: "What impresses an American most, however, is the combination of great joy and spontaneity and activity with equally great self-control and order. The joyfulness is pervasive: in almost every classroom visited, virtually every child appeared happy and engaged. One simply does not see bored or restless or unhappy youngsters, or youngsters with the glazed look so common in American schools." [5]

Silberman also points out that in English formal schools children were restless, in fact they behaved much as children do in most American schools. Thus in commenting on the joylessness of many American schools Silberman also shows that joylessness is not a necessary quality of schools, that it stems not from American national characteristics but rather from the formality and barrenness of schools, characteristics then seemingly have the same effect on both sides of the Atlantic. [6]

It is not easy to account for the dullness and drabness of schoolrooms as places to learn. Part of it has been promoted by universities and schools themselves. These institutions have been extremely bookish. It took anthropology a long time to make the study of living primitive people acceptable. If one studies mummies and other archeological findings no questions are asked. More recently study of primitive societies is seen as scholarly, but study of life in our cities today is still questioned. Some universities have turned their backs on the schools as places to learn something about education, maintaining that more can be learned by theoretical study on campus. One wonders what would be the reaction to a medical school if it proposed to separate itself from hospitals and confined the preparation of surgeons to book study. There is no argument here against theory or theoretical study. We do, however, hold that theoretical study itself is illuminated by the study of living human beings, by the study of life in a community, by actual participation in the living. This is especially true in preparation for teaching

[5] Charles E. Silberman, *Crisis in the Classroom*, New York: Random House, 1970, pp. 228-229.

[6] *Ibid.*, pp. 229.

and educational leadership because teachers and principals have the responsibility for creating a climate for human growth.

Total community education as here defined is more than opening schools
to all, at all convenient hours, in all wanted subjects. If the existing authori-
tarianism and repressive attitude persists in the relation of the school to
the "new pupils" - the parents and the adults - all we will do is to extend
the destructive effects of the worst flaws of existing schoolhouse education.
The adults then become the victims of the same attitudes and practices that
now dull the curiosities and sensibilities of our children. True, the community
school has a program. It sets out to reach all. It offers what interests the people
young and old, and beyond all this, the community school has a spiritual
dimension, a human quality and a very special intellectual outlook.

Consider first the intellectual outlook. Academically minded people often
see an evening program, with such subjects as ceramics and cake decorating
to be anti-intellectual. In community education, we believe the artist to be
as important as the scientist. We believe all human beings have intellectual
capacities . . . that their development is an exciting endeavor. The concept
that learning is fun is central to our thinking about education. Thus, the
community school is not anti-intellectual, it is vigorously pro-intellectual.
It sets out to draw the whole community into the intellectual fold. It does
this by starting with what people want to learn. It knows now from experience
that if one helps people learn today what they want to learn, tomorrow
they will want to learn still other things. We have seen the curiosity of both
children and adults grow. The intellectualism of the community school
is for all.

Our obsession with cognitive learning has somehow dehumanized the
school. We ask the child to give up the life style he has had at home. If he
is black or if he comes from the ghetto, we tell him he must not be the way
he now is. He must be like us: the teacher. This makes him ill at ease.
Of course, young children have a great deal of spontaneity and even the
most repressive teacher needs considerable time to destroy it all. Go into
a first grade - the children look at you when they talk to you, they seem
bright and quite happy. Visit the grades in succession until you get to the
eighth grade. Here all the spontaneity appears to be lost. The children
often look down on the floor when they talk to you. It took more than seven
years, but the job is pretty thorough.

Our present schools have a staggering legacy of pessimism in regard
to the potential of many children, especially disadvantaged children. Also,

33

when the child behaves badly there is a tendency to let this behavior operate as an umbrella over the whole child, that is, we assume the child has less potential for learning because we do not like his behavior. Low estimates of human potential upon the part of the teachers, principals, and directors of a community school has an even more disastrous effect, since the purpose of the community school is to educate the entire community. Often parents and other adults have been away from school for years. Often their own school experiences are not pleasant in retrospect. They are hesitant about approaching educators, doubting their own abilities and skeptical of the educator's willingness to understand them. All of this suggests that personnel selection for the community school is a highly important aspect of developing a successful program of community education. This problem is dealt with more fully in Chapter Nine.

CHAPTER III

THE GIFT
OF
THE DISADVANTAGED

The Gift
of the Disadvantaged

INTRODUCTION

The nation's encounter with the problems of educating the disadvantaged, especially in the inner cities and the remote rural areas, has been an effective testing ground for traditional American education. It is a vivid mirror in which we can see not only our stark failure with the disadvantaged, but also the basic flaws in our usual educational assumptions which would need to be changed even if the disadvantaged were not here, or constituted no problem. In fact, history may record that the children of America have received or will receive a gift from our inner city children, a gift in the form of a better education which can now be provided because of what we are learning in working with the disadvantaged.

Some writers have held that the Negro in America would be the salvation of America, that the Negro would force Americans to face up to their heritage, to ask themselves if they really believed what they say about freedom and about equal opportunity. In the same way, the disadvantaged can be the salvation of American education. For it is here in relation to the education of the disadvantaged that education is tested and the test has not passed. In relation to the poor and the disadvantaged, we have failed. Moreover, if we study the failure we can see why we failed. As we study the reason for these failures, we discover weaknesses in our education which are most assuredly limiting the development of other pupils, even of those with high grades and diplomas.

A CHALLENGE TO EXISTING ASSUMPTIONS

Grant me the assumption and you give me the argument.

Let us consider the implicit assumption that school is intrinsically good for all children. We find inner city children entering school somewhat below national norms on tests, but not as much below as might be expected in view of the disadvantages they have endured. They seem to hold their relative position through the first three grades of the elementary school and begin to drop lower and lower with each succeeding grade. Not only their relative achievement drops, their scores on intelligence tests also drop. Through the years of the elementary school and the first year or two of high school, they learn that they cannot learn. To learn that one cannot learn is to suffer damage that is hard to repair. In past years, many of these children would have dropped out before their faith in themselves had been destroyed. They are now forced to remain in school even though school experience is not relevant to them and failure becomes a persistent experience. It is clearly evident that school experience, in its present form may often be damaging to his self concept.

Another assumption is that failure is inevitable for a fixed proportion of children. Many children are adjudged ineducable. When the child starts school he must learn to read, regardless of his earlier experience and readiness to learn to read. When he sees no reason to learn to read, he does poorly. He gets a low mark, and years of low marks and poor work tell him that he and school "do not mix". He develops a poor self image, becomes more and more alienated, may become unemployable, and even turn to delinquency and crime. He develops a feeling of bitterness toward the school and the whole social order because he feels that he has been reduced to a position with something less than human dignity.

One does not study education very long before one begins to realize the difficulties that children face. The basic assumption that education is a contest in which winning for some means losing for others, leads to a school which is a selective agency rather than an educational enterprise. Various grouping methods which deny slow learners the stimulus of the presence of other children who learn faster, the deadly marking system, the teacher whose attention is on the subject matter rather than the individual child, the conflict between the rigidities of the graded school and what we know about child growth and development—all these, create a setting in which the education of *all* the children is well nigh impossible.

Most of us in education finally come to condone failure. At some levels and in some situations, we even set out to produce it statistically. It is a well-known fact that a university which raises its entrance requirements often continues to fail as large a proportion of the highly selected student body as it did with lower entrance requirements. Success is no longer enough. Students not only get into difficulty by not doing well, but also go down when they do well, if others do better.

One cannot help but be impressed by the persistence with which schools adhere to traditional practices that have been invalidated by research. Surely we know by now that children do not grow in the orderly fashion that is assumed by the graded school organization. Rates of growth are highly variable from child to child. Can it be that we still think the traditional marking system is an aid to learning when studies and wide experience have shown that it destroys the self image of children and alienates them to all schooling?

How can we explain the spread of tracking systems and patterns for ability grouping when those who study the problem can find no kind of grouping that helps children to learn? Are educators ready to admit that adherence to grouping by ability is proof that they do not want to teach individual children but insist on mass methods? Is the system concerned with teacher convenience and comfort rather than child growth?

The encounter with the disadvantaged is calling into question the whole structure and functioning of teacher education. Nowhere can one see the centrality of the teacher as well as in observing teachers at work with inner city children. It is becoming obvious that the primary factors in the success of the teacher are personality, attitude, respect for the child, faith in the child and affection for him. Present teacher education has very little provision for growth of our prospective teachers in these qualities. The concentration of teacher education is on what the teacher should know rather than on what he should do or, even more importantly, what he should be!

It is difficult to see how or when significant change in teacher education is to come about when one realizes that the universities are the big producers of teachers and colleges of education persist in seeing teaching as a science. Education is not a science—it never will be. It is an art. It uses science and we hope will make greater and greater use of science, but it remains an art.

In fact, there is reason to believe that the greater the progress of scientific knowledge applicable to education, the greater artistry the teacher must possess. Massive revised programs in both preservice and inservice education are essential if the new education we need is to become a reality.

Finally, one cannot study inner city schools closely without reaching the conclusion that no matter how we improve the school from 8:30 to 3:30 p.m. we cannot meet the challenges of the disadvantaged. The disadvantaged home has already limited the child. He is already damaged. The damage is cumulative, and the damage at home and in the community exaggerates the damage done by the negative influences of the school itself. If we are to stand any chance of helping inner city children to grow, we must help the parents to improve the home and the community.

It is difficult to understand the reluctance of schools to extend their work to the community. A common teacher lament is the failure of parents; and inadequate homes are at the top of our list of alibis for our own failure. The community school, open from early in the morning until late at night, has existed in places in America for many decades. In theory, education for all runs through the writing not only of specialists in adult education but also in the writings of major leaders in educational program and philosophy. Still the community school is spreading relatively slowly. Our educational leadership somehow fails to sense the problem, and teachers are often indifferent to the program.

Schools are now beginning to take the disadvantaged child out of the home for a few hours in the day to give him some of the experiences which middle class homes provide children. Head Start and other examples of pre-school programs are spreading. Even these desirable innovations lose much of their effectiveness because they affect the child's life for only part of the day. In addition, children who have gained through an experience in Head Start seem to lose the gain in the years that follow in the early grades which continue to provide a climate ill-adapted to the needs of the deprived child. Again we are learning through our confrontation with disadvantaged children. We find that educational changes must not be piecemeal. It is not enough to limit change to early childhood education. All education must be changed.

Unfortunately, most educational research deals with narrow factors and skills concerning minor changes in procedure in an effort to separate specific elements. We do not know how all of the specifics relate to one another. The child's whole life experience is more than the sum of all the activities in which he has been involved. The more than half-century of molecular educational research carried on as described above has yielded very disappointing outcomes. We will not do better until we sense that it is the child's whole life that educates him and therefore when we seek to change this life we will attack every aspect - "pull all the stops". Here we would be following what is general practice in the art of medicine.

PROFILE OF THE DISADVANTAGED CHILD

Who are the "culturally disadvantaged", "culturally deprived" or more accurately, "culturally different", since, technically speaking, everyone has a culture? Kerber and Smith define the "culturally different" as those handicapped in their social competency and cultural functioning in our modern complex society.

> *In general, these children do not know enough of our cultural heritage, do not have the possessions, rewards, competencies or knowledge which are too much taken for granted as given everybody in the American society. He comes from a blighted segregated or socially disorganized area. His family has little education and are often hostile and abusive. The socio-economic status of the home is low. Employment and money to pay bills are constant insecurities. The cultural traits of home and neighborhood . . . the arts, ideational resources, social organizations and recreational outlets and esthetic surroundings are squalid and inadequate. The cultural environment conditions him to violence and degradation. He has few opportunities to experience the meanings of the spoken American ideals.*[1]

The disadvantaged are not easily recognizable by superficial observation. The stereotype of economic deprivation that pictures these children in rags, unclean and unkempt, is not valid. Harrington,[2] in his book, *The Other America*, has observed that the poor are not easily identifiable because mass production has made it possible for most to dress in a similar fashion. The children of inner city come to school as kindergarteners having many of the outward physical appearances in the way of dress and grooming that one characteristically thinks of as middle class American. However, the most casual observation of the neighborhood from which they come

---

[1] August Kerber and Wilfred R. Smith, *Educational Issues in a Changing Society*, Detroit: Wayne State University Press, 1964, p. 155.

[2] Michael Harrington, *The Other America*, New York: MacMillan, 1962.

41

reveals the disproportionate emphasis placed on outward personal appearance. In some schools, particularly in the South, students do dress in a manner more closely akin to what is commonly thought of as characteristic of the socially-economically deprived. There also seems to be a decline in the outward appearance of these youngsters as they progress toward the sixth grade. The ability of the parents to clothe their children in a middle class fashion, beginning with kindergarten, seems to decline as the children reach a later elementary level. However, with the exception of a few cases, the disadvantaged remain invisible with regard to personal appearance.

The recognizable characteristics of the disadvantaged must be defined in terms of limited cultural backgrounds, and a marked difference in ethnic and racial values that act as deterrents toward success in school. The achievement of pupils can be defined in fairly specific terms, showing relationships that are definitive. Sexton[3] presents data that demonstrates conclusively that educational achievement and success in school are directly related to economic well-being. In other words, there is a direct relationship to education and income. This was evidenced by the achievement scores of elementary students in urban areas.

"The composite scores for the major income groups show that, without exception, achievement scores rise with family income levels."[4]

The school, then, has the responsibility for developing techniques that will eradicate the difficulties that are inherent for the children from low-income homes.

Achievement and Intelligence Characteristics

There are significant differences between individuals in any class or school in the core areas of our cities. Demonstrated differences are evident in behavior patterns, motivation, intellectual capacity, academic abilities, and reading abilities. The difference in reading abilities are particularly significant. However, all performance appears to be lower than the norm for any given grade, and the range for all pupils repeatedly appears in the lower quartile.

The type of competition for academic excellence commonly associated with middle class schools is absent. Stimulation seems to be absent and models

---

[3] Patricia Sexton, *Education and Income: Inequalities of Opportunity in Our Public Schools,* New York: Viking, 1961.

[4] *Ibid.,* p. 27.

of high achievement are not common. Beginning students with better than average ability and who have none of the earmarks of the disadvantaged soon begin to develop characteristics of the low achievement group. Scores on measures of scholastic aptitude experience a systematic decline for all but a few children in this environment.

Kenneth Clark, writing in *Education in Depressed Areas,*[5] indicates that teachers often point to low intelligence as a reason for low achievement. Sexton also discusses this problem.

> *But as we said before, there is not a shred of proof that any of these IQ tests are valid measures of native intelligence, and in fact there is much proof that they are not. Yet despite the cautions given by the psychologists who devise the tests, they continue to be used in the schools as accurate measures of native ability.*[6]

This relates to Sexton's study of social class and income.

> *Social class is also a fairly accurate predictor of success in school. If you know a child's class status, his family income, his parent's educational levels, you can quite accurately predict what will happen to him in school and how successful he will be.*[7]

Education has been viewed generally as the driving force and fluid of upward mobility. However, it is in danger of becoming society's sorting agency which "cements" the childs present condition rather than permits and encourages upward mobility.

The Home Environment

Riessman's study, *The Culturally Deprived Child,*[8] characterizes the family of the culturally deprived child as one that is devastated by divorce, desertion, death and economic insecurity. These families live in inadequate

---

[5] Harry A. Passow, *Education in Depressed Areas*. New York: Teachers College Press, Columbia University, 1963, p. 142-161.

[6] Sexton, *op. cit.*, p. 40.

[7] Allison Davis, *Social-Class Influences Upon Learning*. Cambridge: Harvard University Press, 1948, p. 41.

[8] Frank Riessman, *The Culturally Deprived Child*. New York: Harper, 1962.

and overcrowded housing facilities and in an atmosphere where gross punishment is used to maintain discipline. The family is also characterized by many parent substitutes.

> *The home typically includes aunts, uncles and grand parents, all of whom may, to a degree, play a paternal role. In the Negro family, the grandmother often plays a decisive role.*[9]

Riessman also mentions that the lack of satisfactory parental relationships is significant. There is evidence that this is a common pattern in the environment of the underprivileged child.

> *To think of the underprivileged family as consisting of a father, mother and children alone is to miss vital aspects of this family today. Intense parent-child relationships are infrequent, and while the danger of parental rejection is present, over-protection is out of the question.*[10]

David and Pearl Ausubel find that:

> *Even more important perhaps as a cause of Negro education retardation is the situation prevailing in the Negro home. Many Negro parents have had little schooling themselves and hence are unable to appreciate its value. Thus, they do not provide active, wholehearted support for high level academic performance by demanding conscientious study and regular attendance from their children. The greater frequency of broken homes, unemployment and negative family atmosphere, as well as the high rate of pupil turnover, are also not conducive to academic achievement.*[11]

Motivation and Aspiration Characteristics

The findings of Miller and Swanson[12] indicate that motivational differences between children of middle class parents and those of children from

---

[9] *Ibid.*, p. 36.

[10] *Ibid.*, p. 37.

[11] David and Pearl Ausubel, "Ego Development Among Segregated Negro Children", *Education in Depressed Areas*, ed., Harry A. Passow, New York: Bureau of Publications, Teachers College, Columbia University, 1963, p. 124.

[12] David R. Miller and Guy E. Swanson, *Inner Conflict and Defense*, New York: Holt, Rinehart and Winston, 1960.

lower classes are quite apparent to even a casual observer of the children of the inner city. The children of inner city seem to be more "present" oriented rather than "future" oriented. In addition, there seems to be a lack of significant motivational models for these children to copy. Observers and teachers are repeatedly made aware by immediacy of the needs of these children and their unwillingness to forego present rewards in anticipation of future rewards or advantages.

The educational aspirations of the pupil in the lower elementary grades in disadvantaged areas are often high, but disappear by the sixth grade level and that much of the hope and optimism has disappeared and is replaced by apathy. Miriam L. Goldberg sees the following pattern among children from socio-economic deprived homes.

> *Although some may view formal education as desirable it is not vital for job-getting or retention; physical strength and manual skills are more highly valued. In general, self-control and responsibility are less evident and there is more concern with pleasures of the moment than the unknown rewards of the future.*[13]

The school, in the light of these significant factors, needs to consider them if a satisfactory school experience is to be provided.

There is a surprising unawareness of the occupation of the father for students in the third and fourth grades, with a reluctance to discuss occupational roles of parents in later elementary years. The educational and achievement aspirations are often unrealistic for many of these children. In some respects they are without hope. The real tragedy is not that they are disadvantaged at present, but that many, as early as the sixth grade, have abandoned hope for the future.

Peer Relations

The importance of the peer group for the children of inner city at a very early age is one of the striking characteristics of the culturally deprived. One senses that these students are trapped in a dilemma that is characterized by a premature acceptance of their peer group in shaping their attitudes and feelings but soon find this association of peers to be unrewarding. Many studies point to the extra-ordinary importance of peer relationships for these

[13] Miriam Goldberg, Education in Depressed Areas, ed., Passow, *op. cit.*, p. 80.

students at a much earlier age than is experienced by middle class youth. A power vacuum appears to exist which should be utilized by educators. Among deprived children, the age mates assume such an important role in the socialization process that the parents are a poor second in importance, if they are not rejected altogether. The paradox is that these children evidently turn to their peers for acceptance, recognition and identification, and exclude adult leadership. Yet, they are not happy with their plight. It becomes readily apparent that these youth have turned to their peers for self-fulfillment of their basic needs, but since all possess the same need, there is no source to meet the need. Hence there is a lack of fulfillment and the resulting frustrations affect the classroom behavior. Their needs are prolific.

They are starving for adult recognition and the school has not met their needs. Rather than fulfilling needs, the school has tended to erode and in some cases destroy their self esteem. They cannot meet the demands of the adults who represent the school. Consequently, we find the premature reliance on peer approval and acceptance which is equally frustrating. They look for adult acceptance and recognition, but, despite the efforts of a few significant people in every school with whom these youth can identify, all but a few are forced to retreat into their "peer jungle" where hopelessness, hostility and an all embracing rationalization against society takes place.

TEACHERS OF THE DISADVANTAGED

The schools in the core of the city have a reputation for being difficult. Teacher turnover is high. Young teachers out of college are not attracted to working in these areas. Those who stay and are successful are putting forth truly creative performances in view of the multitude of problems that confront the teachers of inner city. Teacher attitudes regarding the intellectual capabilities of their students seem to be the very essence of the problem of the disadvantaged in relation to their success in school. If teachers perceive individuals as having fixed innate intellectual potentialities, we can expect them to treat the entire educational experience as one limited by external predisposed circumstances over which they have no control. Conversely, if they accept the concept of human potentiality as a changing pattern influenced by environmental factors, we can expect the teaching process to take on new dimensions.

Teachers in many of our public schools do not appear to have accepted the premise that an individual's self emerges from interaction with his society

46

and that all he is or ever will be depends upon this interaction. These teachers continue to use methods and techniques that are traditional and expedient. Yet, these are in direct violation of the principles of self-discovery and self-realization for their students. The implications that an individual is what he is because of his interaction with society, has significant implications for the education of all children and major significance for the children from culturally deprived environments. A teacher holding to a belief in fixed innate capabilities often finds the raw material to work with in middle class school environments, but this is seldom the case in the heart of inner city.

Expectancies of Teachers

Many of the teachers of inner city youths are disappointed with the situation in which they find themselves. It appears to be a disappointment in their expectations of what teaching should be. Most teachers enter the field in search of an opportunity to make a contribution to society, and in turn, hope to reach some type of fulfillment in their personal lives. With these expectations in mind, armed with the old cliche "kids are kids", they have entered this totally different type of environment to find that the students are not prepared socially, emotionally or intellectually to benefit from what they have to offer in the way of academic stimulation or personal experience.

Subject-Matter Orientation

Students in the core city are working below acceptable academic standards at all grade levels. There is an apparent need for compensatory educational consideration if we are to reach these children. In spite of these obvious deficiencies, we have repeatedly observed teacher reliance upon traditional methods, materials and psychological theories of learning. Some teachers insist upon the memorization of materials, such as the names of all the state capitols, and the like. Only rarely does one see materials or methods geared to the unique problems these children pose for education.

Attitudes Toward Discipline

Discipline, keeping order and authority appear to be the greatest single concern of teachers in an inner city setting. The concern increases as the grade level advances. There appears to be a constant struggle between the teacher and several members of each class for domination. The struggle takes on the proportions of a war in some instances, and like all wars is all consuming, leaving little time or energy for anything else. Many of the teachers are simply overwhelmed by the classroom complexities brought on by the out-of-school environment of these children.

Colin Greer in a volume entitled *Cobweb Attitudes, Essays in American Education and Culture* makes the following statement:

> *From 1890 at least, the schools fail to perform according to their own as well as the popular definition of their role. In virtually every study undertaken since that of Chicago schools made in 1898 more children have failed in school than have succeeded, both in absolute and relative numbers.*
>
> *The educators who collaborated on the Chicago study found an exceedingly high incidence of poor school performance. They were quick to look to foreign birth as an explanation but immigrants spawned Americans and still with each passing decade no more than sixty per cent of Chicago's public school pupils were recorded at normal grade level, the rest were either over age, one to two years behind or retarded, three to five years behind. In Boston, Chicago, Detroit, Philadelphia, Pittsburgh, New York and Minneapolis, failure rates were so high that in not one of these systems did the so-called normal group exceed sixty per cent while in some instances it fell even lower to forty-nine per cent in Pittsburgh and thirty-five per cent in Minneapolis. The assumption that extended schooling promotes greater academic achievement or social mobility is however, entirely fallacious. School performance seems consistently dependent upon the socio-economic position of the pupil's family. For example, of high school graduates who ranked in the top fifth in ability among their classmates, those whose parents are in the top socio-economic status quartile are five times more likely to enter graduate or professional schools than those of comparable ability whose parents fall in the bottom quartile.*
>
> *Similarly while American males born after 1900 spent more years in school than their nineteenth century predecessors, federal and other estimates indicate no concomitant redistribution of economic and social rewards.*[14]

On a scale of nine semesters, Philadelphia high schools lost sixty-five per cent of incoming students at the end of the first semester, lost another

---

[14] Colin Creer, "Public Schools: The Myth of the Melting Pot", *Saturday Review*, Nov. 15, 1969, pp. 84-86.

thirty-two per cent at the end of the fourth, and were down to nineteen per cent of the total in the final semester. In one instance, in a 339 pupil sample established for survey purposes, only 91 survived two years.

The striking thing about the failure of our schools is the fact that failure is concentrated heavily with the children of the poor. Again, if the poor are scattered among a great many middle class people and their children are similarly included with middle class children, the magnitude of our failure with such children is lost. When a school or an entire classroom is made up entirely of disadvantaged children within this lowest group, the effect is overwhelming. This is what has happened in the inner city and it is for this reason that disadvantaged children concentrated in the poor areas of our cities have made a great gift to all American children. This concentration has alerted us to our widespread educational failure.

One reason we are so slow to sense the weaknesses of our education is that our standards for excellence are so very low. If children enter school at age six and promoted regularly from grade to grade, enter high school, graduate from high school and go to college or into good jobs, the average teacher or lay citizen tends to see this as a successful school system. No one stops to consider whether the education these children have received has really developed them to the fullest extent. True, they have made academic progress regularly. They have graduated and have a diploma and other credentials. This fact, however, has little to do with the question of the extent to which these same young people have become all they are capable of becoming. Business men complain that high school graduates cannot spell, write a decent sentence or a well-integrated paragraph. The vast majority of our children learn to read but only a small proportion are discriminating in their reading or maintain effective reading habits during later years.

THE IMPACT OF CONCENTRATED DISADVANTAGE

Had it not been for the concentration of disadvantaged people in the core of our large cities it is entirely possible that the weaknesses of our educational system would have gone uncorrected for many more decades. We have always realized that there were failures, but in a reasonably well-distributed population such as is found in one of our smaller towns, the failures are relatively small in number and are seen generally to be the fault of the individuals themselves. Concentrate hundreds of thousands of disadvantaged people in the inner city and one begins to see a colossal failure.

This failure is perhaps a little different from failures in our small towns but by bringing them all together in one place in one school or in one schoolroom they make a very striking picture of our inability to educate.

In a classroom that has a wide distribution of children's abilities, the averages and other measures of central tendency show up as being adequate. Little attention is given to those individual children who fall below the average and perhaps even less to those who fall in the lowest five per cent. When the children of low income families are concentrated in one place, the stark reality of our failure cannot be ignored or denied. For example, it is not very alarming to most people to point out that five per cent of the children in a particular schoolroom fail. It is much more disturbing to report that an entire school falls from one to three grades below the average achievement of American children.

SUMMARY

American schools have never been successful in educating the poor. When poor boys occasionally attained distinction, this blinded us to the fact that the vast majority fell by the wayside without education. Also the fact that great leaders have sometimes come from poverty has led us to believe that the American school system was highly productive in bringing about social and economic mobility when the facts are quite the contrary. The whole idea of the school as a "melting pot" is indeed a myth.

Now with the accumulating data concerning the schools' failure with the disadvantaged, there is for the first time a possibility that we will look critically at the entire educational enterprise, examine it in detail and discover the places where it is weak. We know, for example, now that "self-image" plays a large role in the child's capacity to learn. This area is dealt with elsewhere in this volume. We know that teacher attitudes are highly significant in creating a climate for learning. This area is also considered at some length elsewhere. We are learning from day to day that the child's life is a potent factor in influencing his capacity to learn. Our experiences with the disadvantaged are laying the foundation for the development of a whole new educational policy for America, a policy which probably would not have come into being were it not for our encounter with the disadvantaged.

Most important of all, it is difficult to explain the rising incidence of crime and delinquency, drug abuse and widespread social and business irresponsibility among those who have achieved higher levels of schooling. The public as a whole is skeptical, has a feeling that something is wrong but does not know quite what to do about it. Because we have such a concentration of disadvantaged people in our inner cities we have become aware of educational problems that might have gone without attention for additional decades.

Our awareness of inner city problems has resulted in attempts to explain our failure. We have assumed that our failure with the poor is a recent development and that our earlier efforts were more effective with the disadvantaged. These assumptions are incorrect. The opposite is true. Ineffective as the schools are with children in low income areas today, they were less effective a half-century or more ago.

CHAPTER IV

NEW ESTIMATES OF HUMAN POTENTIAL

New Estimates
of Human Potential

INTRODUCTION

The history of man can be viewed as man's struggle to discover his own potential. Dictatorial governments have little faith in the average human being, in his capacity to govern himself and to develop his own criteria of truth and value. Similarly, teachers have been slow to sense the average person's capacity to learn, and many have assumed that a considerable proportion of the children are ineducable. Even though democratic societies rest on man's capacity to learn—on his improvability—teachers and other educators have been reluctant to apply society's basic outlook to the schools. In general, the educational measurement movement has appeared to support elitist views of man's potential. More recently, however, the so called Third Force psychology has tended to make new and more generous estimates of man's potential and more recent leaders in the measurement movement have warned against making unwarranted assumptions concerning the meaning of test results. The net effect has been to provide a more hopeful outlook for human growth through education.

> *When we treat a man as he is, we make him worse than he is. When we treat him as if he already were what he potentially could be, we make him what he should be.*
>
> Johann Wolfgang Goethe

NEW ESTIMATES OF HUMAN POTENTIAL

The most dominant note in the last half century of the history of education has been the measurement movement. More than any other influence, it has determined educational policy and program, shaped the nature of educational inquiry, determined the philosophical orientation of teachers and given the teacher the most powerful estimate of human potential. As such, it has provided the apparent scientific foundation for educational selectivity, for our marking system and most important for the justification of the teacher's failure to help the child to learn. In other words: Accept the premises of the measurement movement and you accept the idea that equality of educational opportunity is unattainable.

The above indictment does not, of course, include all measurement specialists since some have not only been aware of the many pitfalls in the use of their data but also have repeatedly warned against such dangers. The movement has to be appraised, not only in terms of its techniques, but also in terms of the way teachers and educators generally have used the techniques and the interpretations made on the basis of them. That the same techniques could have been used for different purposes and in more creative ways is freely granted. Here we must deal with reality and the reality is that measurement techniques have too often been employed to defend the educational status quo, to scale down the stature of man and to resist change by attempting to show that biological endowments are lacking for more successful programs. Thus the tests have too often comforted the teacher and the administrator and contributed to the discomfort of the child and the worry of his parents.

Testing has been a powerful control in the determination of what is taught, what is remembered by the learner and what the learner sees as important. Teachers teach for the tests, consequently, they teach what their experience has taught them and what the tests usually call for. In other words, we tend to teach what can be measured. Since the tests usually come with regularity in the various grade levels, teachers are afraid of slower learning paces for children, even if they know that for an individual child it would be better for him to learn to read at age seven rather than at age six.

Test construction tends to emphasize the memorizing of facts and also particular kinds of facts, taxonomies and classifications. A film or field trip may enrich the study of history but may not help the children pass tests, so teachers drill their students on the facts and postpone or eliminate the enrichment.

Probably the most negative effect of the measurement movement has been to whittle down the image of man. The bell shaped curve with its small percentage of gifted, its large portion of average children and its small percentage of dull children somehow leaves people with the feeling that dullness is the most common quality of man, that the really important section of the human population is the upper fifteen per cent. It is therefore easier to get support for the education of the gifted than for the average or below average children. Closely related is the notion that very bright children will be held back if grouped with average children, hence the emphasis on tracking and ability grouping.

At this point consideration must be given to the validity of our measures when it comes to selecting our most promising children. The cultural bias of the tests is too well known to need further elaboration here except to point out the handicap faced by the disadvantaged. Most, if not all tests concentrate on verbal and mathematical skills. Since the child's placement is determined by his performance on these tests, it is easy to see how the tests favor the children whose capacities lie in mathematical and verbal directions and discriminate against the children whose talents lie in arts and in human relations.

Test experts will be quick to point out that a child's intelligence quotient should not be seen as a measure of the total worth or promise of the child but this is what it too often becomes in practice. The dangers to justice and to individual children are all the more apparent when we consider the evidence as to the correlation between measured intelligence and creativity.

It is clear that such tests cannot be relied upon to select the children with the highest total promise to themselves and to society. Tests should not be used to determine creativity, innovative capacity, leadership or talent in the arts. Nor can we depend on school marks which are measures of the same abilities as those measured by intelligence tests. The realities we face are that we do not know enough to play God. We don't have the predictive tools. When we try to play God with the tests we have, we can make costly and irreparable blunders. Countless numbers of children have already suffered from extending the meaning and specific validities of our measures beyond that which is justified.

More and more psychologists are viewing intelligence tests as measures of achievement rather than potential. They measure what the child has done with his endowment under the conditions of his environment, but they do not predict what he will do in the future, nor do they indicate what he would do under a changed environment.

Third Force psychologists have injected another element into the whole area of the study of human potential. They point out that few if any of us use very much of our native endowment. This means that if those with less ability can be inspired to great effort to use a large proportion of their capacity - they can achieve whatever is necessary for success in most fields.

For education, such a point of view is dramatic in its impact. It's one thing to teach, to provide education, if the child's native ability is the prime determining factor in his success. It is quite another challenge to teach him if it is assumed that *all* can learn and that the problem is to create the environment that causes the child to use more of his biological endowment.

There is a growing suspicion and some evidence that the testing movement may have been painting far too naive a picture of human capacities and potentials.

BASIC ASSUMPTIONS ABOUT LEARNING AND GROWTH

Routine is a ground to stand on, a wall to retreat to; we cannot draw on our boots without bracing ourselves against it.

Henry David Thoreau

One of the reasons for pessimism with respect to the capacity to learn may be found in our perception of the learning process. Let us view the educational establishment in its entirety and study the scene. One sees lecture halls with elevated desks from which professors and teachers generally make pronouncements, explain ideas and interpret meanings. Students listen as they sit in desks which face to the front and the process of education is expected to proceed. The teacher is the active individual. The students are passive. They are undergoing the process of absorption. Evidently, the assumption is that the more facts they know the better educated they are. It is assumed that there is some mysterious process going on by which listening to these facts and being able to recall them is supposed to produce the educated man.

We know that, except in limited instances, children do not learn in this manner. To be sure, a few students become excited about science and go on to study the sciences leading to doctorates and a lifetime of productive work in science. We know, too, that we are able by this process to produce competent professionals. But those who study professional education comment repeatedly about the lack of general education and broad outlook possessed by our highly-skilled professionals. Meetings of medical, law and engineering schools frequently deal with the question of how these schools can produce broadly educated persons as well as competent experts.

58

We are not without experience in different kinds of learning. It enters into the lives of all of us. We are well-acquainted with the teacher who says that he learned more in his first year of teaching than in all of his undergraduate and graduate study. A returned traveler often feels that his experiences have given him a new outlook on life. The Peace Corps veteran may feel that his year in that organization compares favorably with his four years in the university. These kinds of experiences are significant and exciting because they are experiences in which the individual himself is the actor. He is engaged in the process of developing himself as an individual, expanding his insights, warming his relationships to his fellowmen, coming to understand himself as a person, and acquiring new goals and new perspectives with regard to the ways in which they can be reached.

It appears that we have never faced squarely the task of developing an education in which all the children and students are involved in the process of self actualization. The result is that although we talk about human potential we rarely incorporate the new estimates of human potential into the fabric of the education process. We don't know what people can do by way of self actualization. We know only what we can do to them in lecture halls and classrooms in which the teachers are the active agents. What could children and students do if they became the active agents?

All teachers know that in each class there is a relatively small number of students who seem to move on their own power. There are questions in their minds and they are trying to find answers to these questions. In the process, new questions are being raised. They are learning how to ask the right questions. They seem less concerned with answers and knowledge of facts than with insight and understanding. Teachers find satisfaction in working with such students. Such children escaped the trappings of our educational establishment and came through all the formalized deadening experiences without having their curiosity destroyed or their individuality compromised. It is hard to escape the conclusion that students are what they are today in spite of, rather than because of our system. The rank and file of students have given up the battle.[1] They learned early in life what the teacher wanted. They discovered that when they gave back to the teacher what he wanted they got good grades in school and approval at home and in society generally. They may at times have chafed under the routines but they were willing to pay the price. Generally speaking, they became quite

---

[1] John Holt, *How Children Fail.* New York: Pitman Publishing Corporation, A Delta Book, 1964, pp. 1-181.

skillful in developing strategies that satisfied the wants of the teachers and the establishment. They graduated with good grades in history but rarely read any more history. Many have become proficient in scoring well on examinations on government, but go on to become apathetic citizens.

SOURCES OF DULLNESS IN EDUCATION

The human story does not always unfold like an arithmetic calculation on the principle that two and two make four. Sometimes in life they make five or minus three; and sometimes the blackboard topples down in the middle of the sum and leaves the class in disorder and the pedagogue with a black eye. The element of the unexpected and the unforeseeable is what gives some of its relish to life and saves us from falling into the mechanical thralldom of the logicians.

Winston Churchill

No one can examine textbooks without being impressed with the extent to which these volumes dull the brightness and excitement of whatever subject with which they deal, the outline form in which they are presented, the essentially taxonomic character of the discussion, and the brevity of the treatment. Interesting illustrations from everyday life are often set forth in a pedantic and uninteresting phraseology. The most interesting subject is presented to the child in the dullest possible form. What we see in the apathetic attitude of our students is the student's response to the dullness of the material to which the child is exposed. This dullness continues through all levels of education even through the graduate school. The essential sterility of all of this can be seen especially when areas such as literature, music and art are considered. Here we deal with literary and artistic forms that are intrinsically human in their approach, and yet we can handle these materials in such a way that the student probably can see little difference between what he is studying in the field of literature and what he studies in the field of economics or perhaps in physics. In all of these cases he is dealing with a skeleton from which the flesh and blood and personal meaning have all been extracted.

In every school there are teachers who transcend all of this. Their classes are filled with eager and productive students. These students come out with a new vision of the beauty of mathematics as a language, of painting as an art form or history as a human story with its potential for enlarging our image of man. Such teachers are however exceptional and what is worse, the education we provide for prospective college teachers almost guarantees that we will have very few of them. This surely is not the type of performance we demand of them in their graduate study.

Another aspect of the problem of human potential has to do with the effect of the total environment. It has become crystal clear that the total environment in which human beings grow has a great deal to do with their capacity to learn. We know that children who go to school in the morning without breakfast are not going to be successful in learning. We have ample evidence that children in the inner city and remote rural areas who come from a disadvantaged background achieve less than middle class children. Taken in the aggregate, these experiences suggest that any programs we develop for improvement must attack the problem on a broad front, seeking to alter the entire experience of the individual by changing every possible aspect of his environmental conditions. For example, we know what children can achieve as measured by tests in school subjects in a given school where the school operates from 8:30 in the morning until 3:00 in the afternoon, and where little is done to educate the parents and even less done to improve the homes and the quality of the community. We do not know what these children would achieve if the community were improved, the parents were provided with education, recreational facilities were increased, a well-organized health program were instituted, and changed attitudes of teachers became the order of the day. We judge the potential of human beings by the way they perform under the conditions we have produced for their lives. It does not seem to occur to us that their potential might be changed were these conditions changed.

Too often we explain the slum by charging the people who live there with its production. Some will argue that if slum housing were improved the residents would soon destroy it. We blame the individual human being for every delinquency and every failure. This is a strange shift of attitude from the one we take in the field of agriculture for example. Here we know that good crops can be produced only in good soil. We spend money, time and effort to improve the climate for agricultural products for fruits and vegetables and we are fabulously successful. It is unfortunate that we do not use the same strategy in the determination of policy with respect to human ecology.

Many comments are made about man's inhumanity to man. Equal emphasis could well be given to man's indifference to his own potential and to his own blindness with regard to the wonder of his own creative power. Creativity exists in all children and in all human beings even when they live under distressingly limited circumstances.

TEACHERS PERCEPTION OF HUMAN POTENTIAL

Traditional teachers have much to do with the current general low estimate of human potential on the part of the public. As teachers, we are prone to look for error. We seek the weaknesses of our students rather than their strengths. We celebrate the few who meet our every demand and ignore budding creative talents on the part of those who resist our controls. We prefer girl students to boy students because girls lend themselves more readily to our designs. In general, a good pupil is a child who meets our every wish without protest.

Is an individual low in his ability because his environment is bad or is the environment bad because people are genetically low in ability? Do intelligence tests really measure intelligence? If they do, can capacities be modified by changes in educational experience? These are old questions that have been revived by the present concern with disadvantaged children especially insofar as such children are black. Are black children less able to learn than white children? A recent article by Jensen[2] has provoked much discussion about these questions. There is obviously not space to consider the entire nature-nurture issue at this point. All educators and all citizens must however, be concerned about the conclusions which are drawn from the Jensen viewpoint since they may affect American educational policy determination and American race relations. Were our educational institutions to accept the Jensen interpretation of existing data and base their policies upon them, the result could be a bifurcated school system, one for whites, emphasizing abstract learning and the other for blacks stressing rote learning. The consequences of such a policy for a democratic country can hardly be overemphasized. Martin Deutsch who vigorously disagrees with the Jensen interpretations points out that, "With respect to intelligence testing it would seem that we are deluding ourselves if we believe that such tests truly indicate something about capacity or about general learning ability or that they even reflect the child's current cognitive skills, to say nothing of predicting his potential skills, especially if facilitating stimuli are given. Standard intelligence tests measure essentially what children have learned, not how well they might learn something new."[3]

---

[2] A. R. Jensen, "How Much Can We Boost IQ and Scholastic Achievement", *Harvard Educational Review*, 1969, 39, I-123.

[3] Martin Deutsch, "Happenings on the Way Back to the Forum", *Harvard Educational Review*, 39, pp. 523-557.

If one accepts the Deutsch point of view, measures of present intelligence of black and white children are not measures of their genetic endowment but of their achievement to date. It appears, however, that many still believe that current achievements of children are accurate measures of their native endowment. Few students of measurement would today hold to such a view. A more acceptable point of view is that scores on intelligence tests are in effect achievement test scores. The moment this is admitted it becomes necessary to relate the achievement of all children to their background of experience and it is a well-known fact that black children have, at any school age, already been subjected to the debilitating effect of discrimination and other by-products of their experience. Piaget, for example, holds that:

> *Intellectual development is intimately interwoven with the child's experiences: To the dual processes of assimilation and accommodation the child comes to know his world, to incorporate this knowledge and to modify his understanding in terms of new experiences and interactions.* [4]

Deutsch explains it this way:

> *At an early age, children often with considerable intuition and great intelligence learn not to cope with the school situation, not to attend, not to take it seriously. In other words, they find it intellectually non-stimulating, non-motivating and in circumstances where children and teachers come from different social class and caste backgrounds, children are likely to find the interaction as well as the instruction threatening to their ego structures and personal identities. This is true for normative circumstances. It is most objective and descriptive of ghetto situations. Middle class people who work and teach across social lines often are unable to be aware of the negative aspects of the middle class background because of its apparent superiority of the less advantageous background provided by lower class life.* [5]

As teachers and educational administrators, however, we need not wait for a settlement of the Jensen-Deutsch controversy. As teachers, we must always deal with individual children. It doesn't make any difference at any particular moment in relating to an individual child, whether psychologists ultimately prove that the race to which he belongs is inferior or superior

---

[4] *Ibid.*, p. 529.

[5] *Ibid.*

in ability to another race or group. Differences within a particular racial group are, of course, vastly greater than any differences that could ever be shown between races. The use of racial characteristics to predict intellectual and educational performance of any child is rank injustice. This would be true even if these were valid measures. Among the black children of our society there are many who are capable of doing abstract thinking. (Likewise there are many white children who become athletic stars.) To make educational decisions about individual children on the basis of either real or implied differences in the characteristics of groups as a whole can only lead to gross error and injustice. The really important thing for the teacher to keep in mind in working with a child is that the child is a unique person. He has creative potentialities that the teacher cannot possibly know about at any particular moment. A wise teacher will therefore treat every child as if he were a future genius which indeed he may be. Already too many of us in our profession are playing God on the basis of inadequate predictive devices. We have already perpetrated a vast amount of injustice through the measurement movement. Interpretations of studies based upon inadequate data can do an enormous amount of harm if they find their way into the hands of self-seeking politicians, segregationists and others with anti-democratic purposes. As teachers, we may be unable to prevent all of this injustice. But we can see to it that our own lives and our own relationships to children are not affected by premature conclusions and pseudo scientific findings concerning human beings.

There is considerable evidence that all of us as human beings tend to perform in terms of what people expect of us. If teachers generally have the feeling that the children of the poor and the black have less ability and potential than the children of the middle class, naturally their expectations for these children will be lower. When the teacher has low expectations for the children of the poor, these children will naturally achieve less. Thus, the acceptance of unproved conclusions concerning the genetically determined capacities of children of any particular group, rich or poor, black or white, may have a damaging effect on the effectiveness of the educational program. Intelligence tests have done much to influence the expectations of teachers concerning individual children at early levels of their experience and thus condition their educational performance throughout their lives.

All children can learn. They have already proved this before they enter school, by mastering one of the most complex things they will ever master in their entire lives, . . . a language. The important question for the teacher is not whether one child has more potential than another but to what extent the teacher is able to help each child to release his potential. Far too often we are engaged in the business of comparing one child with another. This is a spurious comparison. No two children are alike. To expect them to perform on the same level is to do violence to the personalities of each.

In total community education, we are not concerned with the relative genetic endowment of all the children and all the people of the community. Our primary concern is not whether black children are brighter or less bright than white children, whether the people who live in the slum have less intelligence than the people who live in the well-to-do suburb. Our major concern is to conduct an educational program that can enable all to live together creatively with an improved environment for growth. What we need to be thinking about is our own capacity to produce such an environment! Fortunately, more recent findings concerning human potential suggest that practically all of us can learn and when all do learn the community will improve.

THE INFLUENCE OF EXPECTATIONS

The superintendent of schools in a town of 3,000 people gets into difficulty with his board of education. He resigns under pressure. His place is taken by a young man who listens to all the problems encountered by his predecessor. Aware of the difficulties, the new man expects people to behave as their behavior has been reported to him. He finds increasingly that the reports of his predecessor are right. He finds the situation not to his liking and resigns. After two or three incidents of this kind, the town acquires a bad reputation and becomes a place to avoid. Now comes still another superintendent who likes people. He meets with a cordial acceptance. His behavior toward his Board of Education, the teachers and the citizens is warm, respectful and trusting. He serves for five years and reports that this is a highly desirable community in which to work. It is, of course, basically the same community as the one which had the bad reputation. The real difference lay not in the community but in the difference in the attitudes of the superintendents.

We deal here with a phenomenon that is widespread in human relations. Most teachers and administrators must know that our expectations of other people affect their behavior, yet as one observes professional behavior it appears that many professionals operate as if they had never learned that expectations influence behavior. In fact, the whole structure of the school— the entire establishment follows practices which appear to ignore the role of expectations. The vast structure of testing which tells teachers that numbers of children are lacking in ability is one example with insidious effects. Beyond this, our general tendency to see any low achievement as a measure of the child's potential places slow learners at a marked disadvantage. To get along well in the establishment, the child should have a high initial test score and very rarely slip in his performance. If the child is a "late bloomer", a slow starter, or if his special capacities lie in art, music or mechanics he is at a marked disadvantage.

Our basic attitudes and feelings toward people affect their performance. In our profession, there are many who believe in the worth of all children. They manifest a warm response to all people and consider each to be a person of ability and warmth. They perceive differences as being precious manifestations of uniqueness. They search for interests and abilities. When they find them, they seek still further development. Such teachers consider differences among their pupils as being both natural and desirable.

Can we select such teachers? To what extent can faith in children be developed and increased? How can this be done? This presents a vast area for research, for teacher education and for inservice training.

While great numbers of educators as well as others who work in human relations are convinced that one's expectation for another's behavior can become a self fulfilling prophecy, we are not without experimental evidence. Rosenthal found that when his experimenters were told that their animal subjects were bright, their animals performed in a superior way. When the animals were described to the experimenter as inferior their animals performed in an inferior manner. Rosenthal then reasoned that if animal performance is improved by the trainer's positive belief it might also be true that children would develop faster if their teachers had high expectations for them.

"To anticipate briefly the nature of this new evidence it is enough to say that 20 percent of the children in a certain elementary school were reported to their teachers as showing unusual potential for intellectual growth. The names of these 20 percent of the children were drawn by means of a table of random numbers, which is to say that the names were drawn out of a hat. Eight months later these unusual or "magic" children showed significantly greater gains in IQ than did the remaining children who had not been singled out for the teachers' attention. The change in the teachers' expectations regarding the intellectual performance of these allegedly special children had led to *an actual change in the intellectual performance of these randomly selected children."* [6]

The evidence appears to be conclusive that the attitudes and expectations of the teacher affect the performance of people. Educational leadership is needed to develop in-service training programs and group work that encourages teachers to become aware of this influence.

The authors believe that one's expectation for another's behavior has special significance in community education. We think this is true because our aim is to educate all; children, parents and the public generally. If the community school director, principal, or the teacher believes the parents and the public to be ignorant and incapable of learning, nothing much is going to happen educationally. Lay people are especially vulnerable to negative attitudes. In any case, they have been out of school a long time and are apprehensive about what they can now do. Beyond this, we need the support of the home and the community if what we do in school is to have any effect. The best conditions prevail when both parents and teachers maintain high expectations. When parents develop the feeling that they are inferior and play no part in the education process, they can not make a positive contribution. They, too, need to be supported if education is to flourish.

The inner city is made up of children and parents who have low expectations. The past has not dealt kindly with them. They see no possibility of a better environment. It is here that the principal or community school director has the opportunity to make constructive change. He can do that only if he has a belief in people and assumes the leadership in developing a staff that can take children and adults where they are and assist them in setting and achieving higher aspirations.

---

[6] Robert Rosenthal, and Lenore Jacobson, *Pygmalion in the Classroom,* New York: Holt, Rinehart and Winston, Inc., pp. vii & viii.

CHAPTER V

POWER OF SELF CONCEPT

Power of Self Concept

INTRODUCTION

You see, really and truly, apart from the things that anyone can pick up (the dressing and the proper way of speaking, and so on), the difference between a lady and a flower girl is not how she behaves, but how she is treated. I shall always be a flower girl to Professor Higgins, because he always treats me as a flower girl, and always will; but I know I can be a lady to you, because you always treat me as a lady, and always will.

G. B. Shaw, Pygmalion

The phenomenon of self is the outgrowth of a body of social-psychological theory concerning the analysis of human behavior. For several decades the concept of self has been a significant consideration in the quest for understanding man's development. Until recently, however, little application has been made of this important concept of learning and behavior in the school setting.

Perceptual psychologists, such as Combs, Snygg[1] and others, have emphasized the importance of the individual's perception of "self" in relation

---

[1] Arthur Combs and Donald Snygg, *Individual Behavior*, 2nd ed., New York: Harpers, 1959.

71

to his intelligence or ability to learn. The general hypothesis derived from the "theory of self" is that the functional limits of one's ability to learn are determined by his self-conception of his ability as acquired through interaction with "significant others".

Recognizing the importance of self in all aspects of human behavior, the analysis that follows devotes itself to the particular aspects of self as it functions in the school learning situation. The analysis is based on the postulate that a child acquires, through identification with "significant others", a perception of his own abilities as a learner of the various skills that he is required to perform in the school environment.

In the development of "self", the expectations of others are internalized by an individual and become a part of a conception of self. As an illustration, if a child perceives that he is unable to learn, if his teacher's expectations of him are low, the self-concept of his abilities tend to diminish which, in turn, becomes the limiting factor in the child's future growth and development.

The second, or companion phase of this chapter devotes itself to the phenomenon of self in relation to children of culturally deprived origins. The response of individuals to the psychological and social conditions in depressed urban areas varies widely for obscure reasons. To what extent an inadequate realization of self plays in the aspirations, motivations and attitudes toward school by the children of the disadvantaged is a primary consideration.

The postulate regarding self-concept and the "interaction of significant others" tends to be exaggerated in the deprived sections of our large metropolitan areas. The extremes are exaggerated. The failures seem to feed upon each other. In these areas of cultural deprivation, the concept of self takes on added meaning.

Kenneth B. Clark [2] suggests that many teachers hold the "pervasive and archaic belief that children from culturally deprived backgrounds are by virtue of their deprivation or lower status position inherently uneducable." Clark sees the Intelligence Quotient score emphasis as a "self-fulfilling prophecy." "When a child from a deprived background is treated as if he is uneducable because he has a low test score, he becomes uneducable and the low test score is

[2] Kenneth B. Clark, "Educational Stimulation of Racially Disadvantaged Children", *Education in Depressed Areas*, ed. A. Harry Passow, New York: Bureau of Publications, Teachers College, Columbia University, 1963, p. 161.

thereby reinforced." Teacher attitude regarding the intellectual capabilities of their students seems to be the very essence of the problem of the disadvantaged in relation to their success in school. If teachers perceive individuals as having fixed innate intellectual potentialities, we can expect them to treat the entire educational experience as one limited by external and predisposed circumstances over which they have no control. Conversely, if they accept the concept of human potentiality as a changing pattern influenced by environmental factors, we can expect the teaching process to take on new dimensions.

The acceptance of the premise that an individual's self emerges from interaction with his society and that all he is or ever will be depends upon this interaction, does not appear to be accepted by the teachers of our public schools. The few who accept it continue to use methods and techniques that are in direct violation of the principles of self-discovery and self-realization for their students.

The implication that an individual is what he is because of his interaction with society, has significant implications for the education of all children and major significance for the children from culturally deprived environments. A teacher holding to a belief in fixed innate capabilities often finds the raw material to work with in middle-class school environments but seldom finds it in the heart of the inner city.

HISTORICAL AND PHILOSOPHICAL BACKGROUND

Our early philosophies envisioned educational opportunities for a limited number of people. In many respects, we have attempted to adapt the selective philosophies of the past to the mass educational needs of the present. Our school systems seem to be designed to separate and screen the student body so that only a selected few can pursue the advanced training and education that our society demands of its citizens and leaders.

The convergence between this philosophy of education and the resulting administrative organization of our schools on one hand and our conceptions of learning on the other is worth noting:

> *Although many theories of learning influence our educational process the dominant contemporary conception is a biological or organic one. An examination of the prevalent variety of curricula and conceptions of achievement reveals the concept of intelligence, a presumed measure of innate individual differences in ability to learn various types of behavior, as the primary foundation. The school system has, therefore,*

> *operated to sort students for various types or levels of education on the assumed basis of individual differences in ability to learn various kinds of behavior.*[3]

Brookover[4] further suggests that since many of the contemporary theories of learning are primarily biological theories they posit learning as essentially a function of the biological organism. Such theories tend to disregard the importance of the social context in which learning occurs. These biological theories see the individual as an organism with a certain limited ability or potential to learn a given kind of behavior (a bucket or container concept of learning). Thus, when the individual reaches the limit of his ability, that is, when the bucket is full, he can acquire no further knowledge in that particular area.

Beginning with Wundt, psychologists have tried to understand the nature of human endeavor, the strivings of the individual, without recourse to the concept of self. Wundt found it too tempting for the philosophers and psychologists that preceded him to call upon the mysterious central agency called the "self" or the "soul" for answers to all questions concerning human behavior. He felt that psychology was being held back and handicapped by the philosophical postulates of the self. Few psychologists during the last half century have resisted Wundt's plea for a "psychology without a soul".

Gordon W. Allport[5] depicts all of the current psychological schools of thought regarding man's development as stemming from two diverse philosophical assumptions. He polarizes all thought regarding man's psychological nature, his growth and theories of learning with the Lockean and Leibnitz traditions at respectively opposite ends of a polar concept. John Locke assumed the mind of the individual to be a "tabula rasa" (blank slate) at birth. The intellect itself was a passive thing acquiring content and structure only through the impact of sensation and the crisscross of association. Locke insisted that there can be nothing in the intellect that was not first in the senses. The Lockean point of view is the dominant concept in American thought regarding the development of the individual. Its representatives

---

[3] W. B. Brookover, "A Social Psychological Conception of Classroom Learning", *Unpublished Monogram*, Michigan State University, p. 2.

[4] *Ibid.*, p. 3.

[5] Gordon W. Allport, *Becoming*, New Haven, Connecticut: Yale University Press, 1955, pp. 6-41.

are found in associationism of all types, including environmentalism, behaviorism, stimulus-response and all other stimulus oriented theories of scientific psychology. Although the principle of conditioning was discovered by Pavlov in Russia, the enthusiasm with which it was seized upon and developed by American psychologists shows its close kinship with the prevailing Lockean traditions. Lockean empiricism has certain presuppositions regarding the nature of man's development and growth. First of all, they hold that what is external and visible is more fundamental than that which is not. Secondly, what is small and molecular is more fundamental than that which is large and molar. Finally, Lockean empiricism assumes that what is early is more fundamental than what is late in development.

The Liebnitzian tradition, by contrast, maintains that the person is not a collection of acts, nor simply the locus of acts: the person is the source of acts. To understand what a person is, it is necessary always to refer to what he may be in the future, for every state of the person is pointed in the direction of future possibilities. The active intellect point of view was preserved on the continent with the Gestalt psychology being the most influential version of the active intellect to reach America.

John Dewey and William James both regarded "self" as a necessary concept and pointed out the danger of disregarding the unity that this mental function provided for the individual. William James [6] saw the self as a composite of thoughts and feelings that constitute a person's awareness of his individual existence, his conception of who and what he is.

The modern theoretical framework for a concept of self is accredited to the works of G. H. Mead, a social psychologist and social philosopher. George Mead, whose lectures were published in 1934 by former students and followers in the *Mind, Self and Society*,[7] puts forth his symbolic interactionist theory. The general hypothesis of this theory is that the functional limits of one's ability is acquired in interaction with "significant others". Mead viewed the self as essentially a social structure and the self arises in social experience. After a self has arisen, in a sense, it provides for itself in its social experience. So we can conceive of an absolute solitary self, but it is impossible to conceive of a self arising outside of social experience.

[6] William James, *The Principles of Psychology*, Vol. I, New York: Henry Holt and Company, 1902.

[7] George Mead, *Mind, Self and Society*, Chicago: The University of Chicago Press, 1934.

Applied to the school situation, Mead's postulation regarding the self explains human behavior as an internalization of a person's concept of himself. By taking the role of, or identifying with, "significant others" (parents, teachers, peers), a student acquires a perception of his own ability as a student of the various skills and tasks he is called upon to perform in the school setting. If the child perceives in his social setting that he cannot learn or if he perceives that his "significant others" do not have faith in his ability to learn, his self-concept of his ability becomes the limiting factor in school success and achievement. Paul E. Pfuetze summarizes Mead's doctrine of mind, self and society.

> *Mead's effort was to state a pragmatic philosophy and social psychology, reinterpreting the concepts of mind and self in the biological, psychological and sociological terms which post-Darwinian thought made prominent, but in such a way that makes possible the expression of individual experience without upsetting the social order. He believed that his analysis of self and society did in fact maintain such a balance, and provided the conditions for the development of selves who are both individual and social, "social individuals". While the precursors of this genetic theory of personality and society are James, Baldwin and Cooley, the clearest statement of this "symbolic interactionism" is found in Mead's account.* [8]

> *Mead's starting point is social experience. Men live together in a world of meaning only because there is a prior undergirding social process within which their biologic lives are set. Both rationalism and empiricism have traditionally tended to regard experience as individual, subjective and mental; and the consequent problem of epistomology was to show how starting from such experience an opposite objective world could be grasped. The usual answer was that it could not be done. Mead therefore shifts the starting point, and points out that "my" has no meaning except over "your", that unless there was a social interaction and a common dimension of experience, the notion of individual private experience would be without meaning . . . Individual selves, yes! But not absolute nor exclusive society. The self is a "SOCIAL" self.* [9]

---

[8] Paul E. Pfuetze, *The Social Self*, New York: Bookman Associates, 1954, p. 100.

[9] *Ibid.*

CONTEMPORARY THINKING RELATED TO SELF

Many of the contemporary psychologists, sociologists and educational leaders have accepted and enlarged upon the basic axioms of Mead's concept of self and its social origin. Leaders in the study of self include Snygg and Combs [10] whose book *Individual Behavior* is considered the classic in the field of self perception.

The concept of "interpersonal relationships" is the central theme of Sullivan's [11] theory of personality and his ideas concerning the way in which troubled people may receive psychological help. According to Sullivan's theory, the self is made of "reflective appraisals". The earliest experiences which influence the development of the self are experiences with other people. The child's earliest self-appraisal is in terms of what others think and feel about him. The origins of the "self" are in the hands of "significant others". Gradually the child perceives expressions of approval and disapproval and a "self" is built out of these experiences of approbation and disapproval or reward and punishment. The experiences thus marked by the attitudes taken by other persons are the ones that become incorporated into a self-concept. If the "reflected appraisals" of the child's self are mainly derogatory as in the case of some of our "children without", then the growing child's attitude toward himself will be primarily derogatory. Sullivan sees a close interrelationship between attitudes toward self and attitudes towards others.

> *As one respects oneself so one can respect others . . . If there is a valid and real attitude toward the self, that attitude will manifest as valid and real toward others. It is not that as ye judge so shall ye be judged, but as you judge yourself so shall you judge others.* [12]

The conception of a healthy self-concept are central in the writing of Karen Horney. [13] She sees the self as both a constant and changing phenomenon. It includes the constant nature of the individual plus all that is conditioned by time and space and that is ever changing. The self provides a nucleus on which and around which experiences are integrated into the

---

[10] Combs and Snygg. *op. Cit.*

[11] Henry Stack Sullivan, *Concept of Modern Psychiatry*, Washington, D.C.: The William Alanson White Psychiatric Foundation, 1947.

[12] Arthur T. Jersild, *In Search of Self*, New York: Bureau of Publications, Teachers College, Columbia University, p. 11.

[13] Karen Horney, *Our Inner Conflict*, New York, N.Y.: Norton, 1945.

uniqueness of the individual. In the process of experience, the healthy self adds, assimilates and integrates with its own system that which is essential and authentic, while renouncing what is unessential and harmful.

Because of the importance of individual perception in an individual's selection of who is significant, the study of the concepts of self is also a study in perception.

One of America's leading perceptualists, Dr. Earl Kelley, suggests that:

> *One of the most revealing facts about perception is that it is selective. There are thousands of coincidences in the situations in which we find ourselves at any given point of time. To perceive them all would cause pandemonium. We therefore* choose *that which the self feeds upon. The direction of the growth of the self depends upon those choices.* [14]

He also sees the self as the key to the development of the "fully functioning person".

> *The self consists, in part at least, of the accumulated experiential background or backlog, of the individual. It is what has been built, since his life began, through unique experience and unique purpose, on the individual's unique biological structure. The self is therefore unique to the individual.*
>
> *This self is built almost entirely, if not entirely, in relationship to others. While the newborn babe has the equipment for the development of the self, there is ample evidence to show that nothing resembling a self can be built in the absence of others. Having a cortex is not enough; there must be continuous interchange between the individual and others. Language, for example, would not be possible without social relationship. Thus, it is seen that man is necessarily a social being. The self has to be achieved; it is not given.* [15]

Arthur W. Combs, considered by many to be the foremost authority on the development of self-concept, describes the development of self-concept:

---

[14] Earl Kelley, *Perceiving, Behaving, Becoming: A New Focus*, Association for Supervision and Curriculum Development, N.E.A., 1952, p. 14.

[15] *Ibid.*, p. 9.

The self-concept, we know is learned. People learn who they are from the ways in which they have been treated by those who surround them in the process of their growing up. This is what Sullivan called "learning about self from the mirror of other people". People discover their self-concept from the kinds of experience they have had with life; not from telling, but from experience. People develop feelings that they are liked, wanted, accepted and from having been successful. [16]

Arthur T. Jersild discusses the function of self in development of a whole-some and integrated personality.

The concept of self provides a key to the understanding of mental health. According to the implications of the self-concept, the healthy individual is true to himself. His "real self". He is authentic. He has integrity within himself. His conception of himself, to the extent that he has formulated it is substantially valid. The individual who does not possess good mental health is one who has not succeeded in developing his potentialities or is integrating the experiences of his life in a manner that makes for a unified whole. He is alienated from self in the sense that there are tendencies within him that are incompatible and therefore in conflict. He has a hostile streak. Because he is at odds with himself, he must pretend to be what he is not, play a role, act "as if". And when he lacks authentic and workable standards of his own, he is false to himself by living according to a borrowed or makeshift standard, playing up to an image that is not in keeping with reality. [17]

Both Carl R. Rogers and A. H. Maslow see the lack of self-identity and full realization of the self as major contributors to the problems of individual development. Before a person can become a fully functioning individual, Rogers maintains he must first:

. . . move toward being open to his experience. This is a phrase that has come to have increasingly definite meaning for me. It is the polar opposite of defensiveness. Defensiveness I have described in the past as being the organism's response to experiences which are perceived or anticipated as incongruent with the structure of the self. In order

---

[16] Arthur Combs, "A Perceptual View of the Adequate Personality", ed. Arthur Combs, *Perceiving, Behaving, Becoming: A New Focus,* Association for Supervision and Curriculum Development, N.E.A. 1962, p. 51.

[17] Jersild. *op. cit.,* p. 10.

to maintain the self-structure such experiences which are given a distorted symbolization in awareness, which reduces the incongruity. Thus, the individual defends himself against any threat of alteration in the concept of self by not perceiving those meanings in his experience which contradict his present self-picture.

In the person who is open to his experience, however, every stimulus, whether originating within the organism or in the environment, would be freely relayed through the nervous system without being distorted by a defensive mechanism. There would be no need of the mechanism of "subception" whereby the organism is forewarned of any experience threatening to the self. [18]

Maslow lists thirty-nine propositions of growth and self actualization. He outlines the physiological and psychological materials that provide the inner nature, the needs, the capacities, the talents, and the anatomical equipment that influence the development of self.

We have, each one of us, an essential inner nature which is intrinsic, given "natural" and usually, very resistant to change. The inner nature includes hereditary, constitutional and very early acquired roots of the individual self, this is raw material to be reacted to by the person, by his significant others, by his environment . . . this raw material very quickly starts growing into a self as it meets the world outside and begins to have transactions with it. [19]

In summary, the contemporary advocates of self-concept are making an appeal for a modification of the prevailing conceptions of learning in the classroom and in the community. Psychologists, anthropologists, sociologists, social psychologists and educators have a wealth of information and knowledge regarding the social aspects of learning. We have somehow managed to avoid an application of this knowledge to school learning. We know that group differences in Intelligence Quotients reflect the social environment which provides different kinds of learning experiences, and that the intelligence tests are loaded with white, middle class learning and behavioral patterns. But in spite of our awareness of the bias of ability instruments,

---

[18] Carl R. Rogers, "Toward Becoming a Fully Functioning Person", *Perceiving, Behaving, Becoming*, ed. Arthur Combs, *op. cit.*, p. 23.

[19] A. H. Maslow, "Some Propositions of a Growth and Self-Actualization Psychology", *Perceiving, Behaving, Becoming*, ed. Arthur Combs, *op. cit.*, p. 40.

our present educational practices are heavily weighted with the assumptions that stem from the belief in fixed, innate ability and the biological orientations toward learning and achievement.

Dr. W. B. Brookover [20] outlines the basic postulates and assumptions of current thinking about the importance of self-concept and the implications of learning. He has found that:

1. There is no real evidence on the limits of human learning.

2. Granting biological differences and the tremendous range of potential, the limits of individual achievement have not been reached.

3. The human organism has tremendous range of learning possibilities and a great variety of learning opportunities.

4. A child will learn behavior appropriate to his society and culture.

5. Learning is a combination of the individual's biological organism and the impact of social factors in his environment.

6. Nearly all human beings can learn the expected behavior of their society.

7. The process and organic mechanisms necessary for learning culturally required behavior are not significantly different from the process and mechanisms necessary for learning the type of behavior and skills taught in the classroom.

8. Persons learn to behave in ways that they consider appropriate to themselves.

9. Appropriateness of an individual's behavior is defined by each person through the internalization of the expectations of significant others.

10. The functional limits of one's ability to learn are determined by his self-conception or self-image as acquired in social interaction.

These postulates and assumptions reinforce the viewpoint of the authors that education is functional only when the educational environment contributes to the development of the self concepts of those in the learning process.

---

[20] Brookover. *op. cit.*, p. 8.

Education II

IMPLICATIONS FOR THE CHILDREN OF THE INNER CITY

The concepts of self and social implications of learning seem to be especially significant for the children of the inner city. It is in this area that a recognition of the social concepts of learning needs the greatest emphasis. It is here that we must begin to break the grip of the self-made trap that holds us to the belief that intelligence is strictly an innate gift and that we are limited as educators by factors of inheritance.

These social concepts of learning must become an important factor in the educational procedures of the inner city schools if we are to experience any degree of success. The two factors that characterize the children of inner city more vividly than any other are the high incidence of school failure and a general dislike for school exhibited by a high percentage of the older children in this environment.

> *Many children find the educational scene so filled with failure, so full of reminders of their limitations, and so harsh in giving these reminders, that they hate school. School is such a threat to their self-picture that it is almost intolerable, but they drag themselves back to school day after day because the alternative of not going would be even more painful and threatening.* [21]

> *Even where the school situation is about as perfect as a human institution can be, children are likely again and again to be reminded of their failings, shortcomings and limitations. In a good setting such reminders are wholesome, for they help the child to face and to deal with realities of life. The school would be at fault if some miracle of sugar-coating it could give all pupils a false rosy conception of themselves. But there still remains great leeway for unhealthy things to happen. The failures, reminders of limitations, and the rejections which children face at school are often artificial and forced. They may have the effect of humiliating the child by depreciating his worth in a manner that does no good to society and does him great harm. Much of the failure at school is contrived. Much of the depreciating children encounter there is based on false evaluation. Some of it rests upon a punitive approach to education which in some schools has a savage intensity.* [22]

[21] Jersild, *op. cit.,* p. 100

[22] *Ibid.,* pp. 90-91.

The concept of self provides the key to mental health. The individual who does not possess good mental health is one who has not succeeded in developing his potentialities or in integrating the experiences of his life in a manner that makes for a whole person. He is alienated from self. He may be hostile. He may pretend to be what he is not, play a role (the tough guy). He is false to himself. He lives by borrowed and makeshift standards. He plays to the image of others, often not in keeping with reality. He is a victim of the whims of others, most often those of his peer group.

The concept of self is further complicated in the culturally different environment in that a person will go to extreme lengths to protect, vindicate and defend a position of self. Thus, while the self is a continuously growing and changing phenomenon, it is also paradoxically strongly geared to prevent growth and to resist change. A person will use every possible psychological defense mechanism to preserve his self-hood, even though it is based on false premises. Dr. Earl Kelley's [23] observations on perception, its selectivity and the fact that people "choose that which the self feeds upon", has very significant ramifications for the children of the culturally different. The problem then becomes one of assisting the learner to accept change without damage to his self image.

[23] Kelley, *op. cit.*

CHAPTER VI

EDUCATION THAT CAN MAKE THE DIFFERENCE

Education That Can Make The Difference

INTRODUCTION

Everything has been thought of before, but the difficulty is to think of it again.

Goethe

As one reads the press about violence in the streets, watches the television reports of disorder on the various campuses of our universities, notes the increase of crime and what appears to be growing disrespect for law one can easily lose sight of the true human grandeur of America. Ours is the oldest continuing free government in the world. Our society has brought prosperity and well-being to three-fourths of our people. Seen from the vantage point of a pre-first World War year, our record in reducing poverty alone is beyond the fondest expectations. In the world of science and technology America leads the world.

More important than any specific achievement is a state of mind. In America we have hope, we have optimism, we believe that things can be changed. We think hard problems can be solved. For this note of optimism which has characterized most of our history we must give credit, in part, to our rich natural resources and to the great talents of our people. As a people, our talents have been enriched by all ethnic groups. The most constant ingredient of our future-oriented outlook is education. We have always had an almost mystical belief in the power of education. Part of our folklore is the notion that any young person can rise to the highest level in our economy through education.

In the last decade doubts about the effectiveness of education as a social and economic escalator have been growing. Much is said about the problems that surround the school: the violence breeding metropolitan apartheid, the incendiary anger that exists among the "Have nots" of our urban areas, the crippling limits that environment places on children from poverty stricken homes. American cities are becoming physically, psychologically and economically bankrupt. To even the most casual observer, it should be evident that the present system of education is not up to the challenge and that the situation is steadily worsening. Advocates of reform often prescribe larger and more frequent doses of the time-honored remedies. Programs, policies and approaches that failed initially have little chance for success the second time around. The remedial innovative procedures often take on a Rube Goldberg quality; one innovation piled upon the other, each focusing on its own peculiar aspect of the process.

Thus, in spite of our historic faith in education, in the face of great quantitative accomplishments, one question still haunts Americans, "what type of education can make the difference"?

If the assumption that many of the failures to meet the needs of children stem from environmental factors outside the school is correct, future educational successes may hinge on the school's ability to cope with community problems rather than on internal reorganization of curriculum and scheduling. If the problems are, in fact, externally oriented, all the internal reorganization and modification that have traditionally characterized school innovation may continue to produce dismal results. Until schools become involved in the community, the total community, and come to grips with the external problems that limit the education of children, our feelings of frustrations and futility will continue and magnify in scope and depth.

EDUCATION I

Like its politicians and its wars, society has the teenagers it deserves.
J. B. Priestly

The way in which middle class America—the "silent majority"—can be so rapidly and deeply moved by the plight of birds in the fields, deer and alligator in the Everglades, giant redwood in California and baby seals in the Arctic, yet can tolerate the more gradual deprivation through neglect (benign neglect) of the human and physical resources of our communities is inexplicable.

The very economic prosperity which the majority of Americans enjoy today tends to blind them to the full meaning of freedom. Things become ubiquitous in the lives of men. In addition, freedom is accepted carelessly. It has always been here. It is not always realized that freedom for humanity wherever it has been enjoyed, has been hard won. It has not occurred to many that most people in the world do not enjoy freedom nor its fruits. The result of all this is that threats to freedom are ignored. It has been said again and again that unless all have freedom none will ultimately have it. If this admonition is taken seriously, one soon realizes that failure to make the American Dream a reality for any section of our population will ultimately hazard freedom for all. Life in the slums with its distrust, despair, envy, and hate is ignored. Since these citizens feel they have a small stake in our present institutions, it is not surprising that some set out to destroy our institutions.

Can education be the escalator that people have popularly believed it to be? The writers, in common with most teachers, believe the answer is yes! Education can make the difference between success and failure for this dream, but it has to be a particular kind of education. It is just not true that schooling is inevitably good, that a little is desirable and that more is better. We know from our experience with disadvantaged children that schools harm some children, that many disadvantaged children would have been better off if they had quit school earlier before the school convinced them they could not learn.

We maintain, in this volume, that education can make the difference if we change many of our old assumptions such as:

1. The present type of schooling is intrinsically and inevitably good, good for everybody and the more years in school the better.

2. Failure for a substantial proportion of the children is inevitable, in fact the price of "high standards".

3. A sizable percentage of children are ineducable and low achievement is the child's fault.

4. Ability grouping facilitates learning, and slow learning pupils in the class cause brighter pupils to achieve less.

5. The marking system motivates children to higher achievement.

6. The graded school facilitates learning.

7. Class size should be the same for all children and teachers.

8. The really important decisions in education should be made by administrators and supervisors.

9. The teacher's knowledge of his subject is the greatest element in his success.

10. A school program from 8:30 to 3:30 p.m. can meet the current challenges to education.

11. Public schools are for children between the ages of 5 through 18 years.

12. A school can divorce itself from the social-economic milieu of the community.

13. That which is similar and measurable is superior to that which is unique and affective.

14. Children and parents are motivated by failure.

15. Low income parents don't care about their children.

16. Education is a terminal process.

17. Children and parents respond best when threatened.

18. Education is the accumulation of facts.

19. Schooling and education are synonymous.

20. Feelings are irrelevant since they are so difficult to measure.

Many have had doubts about most of these assumptions for years, but our experience in the last decade has convinced us that they are all false assumptions. False assumptions inevitably lead to failure. As long as our educational programs rest on the assumptions listed above, such programs will be inadequate no matter how much money we spend on them.

The thesis in this volume is that a program resting on our most common assumptions cannot meet the challenges of modern technological, urbanized America and that an educational revolution is demanded if education is to meet the expectations of the people.

In America we are proud of our education. We have championed the right of every child to an education. Moreover, our education has many great achievements to its credit. The trouble is that a great many of its assumptions, many of its practices, and many of its teacher attitudes have been rendered obsolete by changes in our society. Further, trends in world affairs and recent research concerning the nature of the human organism and human behavior call for an examination of our present efforts. We need a new concept for the educational enterprise. Before outlining roughly such a concept we need to examine assumptions about learning.

BASIC ASSUMPTIONS ABOUT LEARNING

It's nothing less than a miracle that modern methods of teaching haven't completely strangled the delicate process of inquiry.

Albert Einstein

Whenever man has encountered recurring needs he has traditionally institutionalized the servicing of these needs. So it is with education. Society has institutionalized the educational process and refers to it as "schooling".

Institutions and organizations develop life styles and rationales all their own. In a manner resembling a cultural or institutional drift, the establishment pursues a given path, (life styles) without stopping to analyze its purpose and functions in a changing society.

Why Do We Learn

Man learns for many reasons that may briefly be summarized into five categories. The first is that he learns for intrinsic reasons, for the sheer joy of learning. Such as the electrical or chemical impulse that brings visceral pleasure, the tingle in the back of one's neck. The sheer joy of knowing or hearing what one knows triggers and motivates further learning. When the conductor announces that the symphony is about to play the "William Tell" overture, the audience applauds. The audience is not necessarily applauding the performance. They are applauding the fact that they all know the "William Tell" overture. Some educators have lost sight of the "joy of learning", of the intrinsic reasons for learning. The Gestaltists talk about "closure", the need to bring things into "proximity", into "good form". These needs are intrinsic in man's nature. An analysis of current educational theories and educational practices brings to light the apparent lack of concern for the intrinsic motivational factors that are at the very core of man's search for knowledge.

91

Secondly, man learns for "transfer". One of the ironies of the educational profession is the prevalence of misconceptions regarding the term "transfer". To many teachers "transfer" means moving from one school to another and for many educational administrators their only operational concept of transfer is one of being promoted or moved to another job. Transfer in learning is the key notion in learning. As educational planners, if one can't answer the question of transfer, then a reassessment of that which passes on for content is indeed needed. Education is intended to free people, not to enslave them. If content cannot or does not answer the question of transfer for future problem solving of how knowledge can be used in the solution of new problems, then the old notion of schooling, and what constitutes content must be reassessed.

In its broadest sense "transfer of learning" is basic to the whole notion of schooling. One assumption that underlies our entire school system is that learning mastered in school should be applied in some degree to the solution of new problems as they arise in future school and life situations. Consequently, the effectiveness of a school depends in large measure upon the amount and quality of transfer potential of the content that students are expected to learn.

Seen in terms of the above analysis, what is being taught in present schools does not make much sense. How transferable are facts such as "The Imports and the Exports of Bolivia", the "Annual Rainfall of Guatemala", States and their capitals, dates, "1492, 1812, 1819, 1863", and the like. Too often these bits of information make up the content of our schools. Do they represent transferable information that may be applied to future problem solving? Transfer of learning is the cornerstone upon which education should ultimately rest. In essence, when we say that our central aim in education is developing a student's ability to think, we are discussing transfer. Too often, in our present institutions, we have fallen into an institutional drift where we have given an excessive emphasis to memorization. The fact that one can memorize facts does not mean that one is able to use these facts or think with them.

The third reason for learning is that man learns for extrinsic reasons. Extrinsically we learn that which is rewarded and the ways in which we may avoid punishment. We are taught that a gold star is better than a blue star, that a mark of "A" is better than a mark of "F", and that a Bachelor's Degree is to be respected. In this respect we have developed an educational structure that honors extrinsic outcomes of the educational process. It is not uncommon for a student to comment or react to the question: "What did you get out of Ireland's course?" . . . "I got an A." This is testimony for the belief that "that which is honored will be practiced" in an institution or society.

If extrinsic rewards are honored, we should expect their practice. Educators can only demand of others that which they expect of themselves. Too often the teaching profession has seen the ultimate goal in education as the "Degree". Too often the prevailing attitude and value have been passed on to the students. One need not grope for illustrations to point out the fact that the extrinsic purposes have been overemphasized in the present educational structure.

Finally, man learns for survival. Schools are established to perpetuate the society, to provide those skills that are needed for society's survival, for the cultural survival. This does not imply survival in an animal or base sense. Rather, it refers to survival in a society characterized by humanitarian values. Robert Oppenheimer was asked whether man could survive after a nuclear holocaust. He suggested that possibly he might survive but that it would be difficult to recognize him as man. Survival is discussed here in the sense that H. G. Wells envisioned when he defined education as "a race between civilization and catastrophe". Education for survival may be defined as a process through which MAN IS MAKING MAN FOR THE SAKE OF MAN. Mankind has institutionalized its hope for its survival and for its progress in its educational establishment. The survival foundation of schooling is exemplified in Harold Benjamin's "The Sabre Toothed Curriculum", a satire based on the curriculum for survival that refuses to change with changing times and drifts on to become irrelevant and meaningless. The unexamined institution is in constant danger of wandering into irrelevancy and meaninglessness. We have created institutional ruts as well as a mental "Calf-Path".

Calf-Path

One day through the primeval wood
A calf walked home as good calves should.
But made a trail all bent askew
A crooked trail as all calves do.
Since then three hundred years have fled
And I infer the calf is dead.
But still he left behind his trail
And thereby hangs my moral tale.
The trail was taken up next day
By a lone dog that passed that way.

Education II

And then a wise bellweather sheep
Pursued the trail over vale and steep
And drew his flock behind him, too
As all good bellweathers do.
And from that day, o'er hill and glade
Thru those old woods, a path was made.
And many men wound in and out
And dodged and turned and bent about
And uttered words of righteous wrath
Because twas such a crooked path.

But still they followed, do not laugh
The first migrations of that calf.
And thru the winding woods they stalked
Because he wobbled when he walked.
This forest path became a lane,
That bent and turned and turned again.
This crooked lane became a road
Where many a poor horse with his load
Toiled on beneath the burning sun
And traveled some three miles in one.

And thus a century and a half
They trod the footsteps of that calf.

Each day a hundred thousand enroute
Followed the zig-zag calf about
And oe'r his crooked journey went
The traffic of a continent.
A hundred thousand men were led
By one calf, near three centuries dead.
They followed still his crooked way
And lost one hundred years per day,
For this, such reverence is lent,
To well established precedent.

For men are prone to go it blind
Along the calf-paths of the mind.
And work away from sun to sun
To do what other men have done.
They follow in the beaten track
And out and in and forth and back.

And still their devious course pursue
To keep the paths that others do
They keep the path a sacred groove
Along which all their lives they move.

And how the wise old wood gods laugh
Who saw that first primeval calf.

Samuel Foss

As teaching has moved down the unquestioned path, many abuses have been perpetrated on the profession and on the children that are served. Many teachers have simply gone through the outward manifestations of becoming teachers. They place plants on their desks, have something alive in the room, keep grade books, and make sure that the pencil is there for recording neat numbers and precise grades after the name of each student. They give series of tests that require the memorization of meaningless trivia, the purpose of which is to separate students by a predetermined classification system. In most cases, the grading system is derived from the notion that the success of some is based upon the failure of others. Education has historically asked students to memorize information that is not transferable, not relevant, not in keeping with their lives now nor in the future. As a result, students have taken up the chant of "irrelevant" and "meaningless" and show other manifestations of rebellion against the existing institution.

Basically they ask for a schooling that is:

1. Aware of the intrinsic needs of man.

2. Transferrable to today's and tomorrow's world, not a curriculum with one foot in the grave and the other on slippery trappings.

3. Selective in the extrinsic rewards that it honors.

4. Dedicated to survival in the protean age.

What Do We Learn

That which is honored in a society is practiced and that which is practiced is learned. As an illustration, it is rather inconceivable to envision a patron of the Renaissance ignoring a potential genius in the Arts. It would be almost impossible for a young man to make a mark on the side of the wall, or to dab paint on a canvas without someone looking into the possibility of his potential. Today, it is equally inconceivable for a young man to throw a "bullet pass" forty yards or throw a curve ball without being identified in our society. Our society honors football and the curve ball. We also honor the "yes" or "right" answer. John Holt's *How Children Fail*—brings out the inordinate amount of prestige we give to the answer "yes"[1] . Arthur Combs—suggests that we have carried this to the point where "no" answers too often mean failure and we have thus confused mistakes with failure in our schools.[2] All people make mistakes, and some of them are made before breakfast coffee. Most individuals can tolerate mistakes. However, individuals *cannot* tolerate continuous failure yet we have convinced many young people that "to make a mistake is to fail".

Schooling in effect has become a screening system. A system that allows for the right answer and makes no allowances for the wrong answer. This attitude has developed in spite of the fact that we have evidence that:

- Fear of being wrong thwarts learning

- Fear of being wrong stifles creativity

- That process, rather than rightness or wrongness is the essence of learning, particularly in dichotomous situations.

- .333 is a good average in business, industry and athletics

Schools have taught and children have learned that which society honors, and emphasis has been given to that which appears to be rational. Someone once defined a man with "common sense" as one whose feet were on the ground, or one who has his feet next to yours. Individuals have a view of reality or a sense of what is real. Learning in one sense is gathering information that proves an individual's rationality. Men and societies are constantly searching for evidence to prove their rationality. Rationalism had its roots in God but it came about because people needed to explain their beliefs, and their common sense. Science has the facts but what is one to do with the facts? These questions are defined by a rational approach to what is learned. Students, in a sense, are philosophers since they do ask "so what" questions. Individuals are constantly making decisions as to what is good, what is of value, and what is truth. All men, even children, have a selective per-

[1] John Holt, *How Children Fail*, New York; Pittman Publishing Co., 1964.

[2] Arthur Combs, *Perceiving, Behaving, Becoming,* Washington; Association for Supervision and Curriculum Development, 1962.

ception that is philosophically oriented. This philosophical orientation determines what shall come through that perceptual screen. In summary, what is learned depends in no small measure on what the individual and his society is willing to let come through a selective philosophical screen.

Man learns that which he perceives. "Seeing is believing." A more accurate statement is "Believing is seeing". Truth is in the eyes of the beholder. Man develops a psychological selective process, a selective perceptual screen, that allows us to view only those things that will psychologically fit each individual's preconceived notions of what is good, what is truth and what is of value.

An individual will learn that which is necessary for survival in the society that he perceives. Survival and coping skills vary and are constantly changing. Schools were originally formed to teach survival skills. They have taken these survival skills and vastly over-complicated them. The basic notions were relatively simple ideas that have become overly fragmented and complicated due to the loss of insight and cultural perspective. Learning for survival involves four basic concepts:

The development of:

1. A man who has the ability to live with himself, to cope with himself and to face up to who he is and what he is and where he is going.

2. A man who has the ability to live with others. The whole process of interaction and socialization skills fall into this category.

3. A man who can identify the aesthetics. He is aware of something beautiful and recognizes a beautiful object without tripping over it.

4. A man who can cope with his environment. In order, to cope with one's environment today, one must be able to master and work with a complex technological setting.

These four abilities; coping with self, with others, and aesthetic environment and the technological environment are the heart of the educational process. Through departmentalization, fragmentation and specialization, schools have lost sight of the very essence of education.

Finally and most importantly students learn that they can learn or conversely they learn that they cannot learn. This is probably the most important concept that is taught and learned in school or in any learning setting. Readers of this volume have learned one important lesson. You have learned that you can learn. A host of people who have encountered the educational systems have come to an opposite conclusion. They have learned that they cannot learn. They have learned that they are intellectually poor, . . poor - not broke . . again there is an important distinction here. Most of us have experienced times when we were broke. To be broke is to be without money for a time and at a place. To be poor in the real sense, however, is to believe that one is down and going down. It involves loss of hope, of the future or of any alternative. This is what it means to be poor. To believe that one cannot learn is to be poor in spirit. All of us have experienced the feeling of not knowing. In this analogy, to be broke is to "not know". It is to be intellectually broke but not intellectually poor. We have an educational system or more accurately a scholastic structure that is in the process of convincing some children, particularly the children from low income homes that they are intellectually poor and that they cannot learn. The tragedy of our time is that many children accept this diagnosis and also the prognosis of their ability for their future at a very early age. Kozol called it "Death at an Early Age". Believing that they can't learn, they behave as if they cannot learn and become alienated from our society.

> *You seldom, if ever, have an old environment plus a new element, such as a printing press or an electric plug. What you have is a totally new environment requiring a whole new repertoire of survival strategies.*[3]

A NEW EDUCATION

A critical analysis of American education not only reveals the weaknesses of the current educational structure, but also indicates the need for developing a program for effective change. To put into effect what is known, will involve decisions and actions more dramatic than the changes that resulted from the teachings of Horace Mann. First, we must make up our minds about what we expect American education to do. Are we serious about providing an education that can meet the challenge of the American crisis? Do we intend to educate all the children or are we going to limit ourselves to the upper two thirds or three-fourths and leave the problem of unemployability and crime to other governmental agencies? The educational system now dumps a million inadequately prepared youth on the society every year. How long can our people tolerate this waste?

---

[3] Postman and Weingartner. *Teaching as a Subversive Activity*, New York, 1970, Delacorte Press, p. 7.

If our promises to educate all of the children of all of the people are to be more than vain hopes, we have no other choice than to build A New Education. In one sense, there will be little that is really new when we have brought about the required educational revolution. Nearly all the specific elements are now in action in various schools and communities. What will be new is a massive community education effort putting all the pieces together in one place and making them more effective. Teaching and leadership must therefore be based on different assumptions and permeated by a primary concern for what happens to the expectations of children, teachers, parents and the community.

In the new education, leaders will think not only of schools, but also of all the agencies and resources in the community that can make a contribution. All will see the whole community as education centered. The growth and development of children, teachers, and parents will be seen as the community's primary reason for being.

When it comes to schools or any other educational program, they will be rated as good only when they meet the needs of the individual child. The convenience of the establishment, the claims of a school subject, the lure of traditional practices will have a diminished priority for school and educational programs. This nation is rich enough to mount a program that uses all that is known about education.

Failure will not be countenanced. We will hold that all children are educable. High standards in the new school will not be judged by group test scores but in terms of what has happened to the self-concepts of the children. Satisfaction will come only when each child is provided with the climate which helps him to become a producing member of society. Newer and higher estimates of human potential indicate that children of very limited ability can learn more than was once believed.

Children will not be segregated by race, intelligence test scores, nor other such artificial devices. In later life, children will not live in a society structured in that manner. Neither should that structure prevail in schools. A community is not rendered desirable by the uniformity of its people but by their variability.

The current marking system will be banished and the achievements of children will be reported in terms of language that is descriptive of them as persons and the degree to which each child is helped to develop his potential. No ratings which destroy the child's confidence in himself will be used.

The school will be ungraded. Its work will meet the level of development of each child. He may move rapidly or slowly but the work will be so paced that the child can go home every day feeling that he has had a measure of success. Brilliant pupils will not be made to slow their pace to that of others. Slow learners will not be given marks which brand them as unworthy.

A new kind of professional outlook is demanded of the educational profession. In medicine, for example, success seems to reward the physician when he undertakes the difficult tasks, the stubborn diseases and when he devotes himself to the people who need him the most. In education this seems to be reversed. The highest rewards go to those who work with the students who need little help. The teacher seems to seek a kind of ease and comfort in working with clean, fast learning children who acquire a little knowledge and skill if one merely keeps school. As teachers, we dread the hard tasks of the inner city. This is due to the nature of teacher education which is largely subject matter oriented and presents learning with almost no meaningful experience with the disadvantaged.

The uniform teacher-pupil ratio will be abandoned. Some teachers may have twenty-five pupils, others fifteen, others five and some may do only individual instruction. The class size will depend on the needs of the children.

If the changes already indicated are to come about, the administrative organization must be broadened to give teachers decision-making power. The frustration of teachers and principals in our large cities has been adequately documented. In medicine, the important decisions are made close to the patient by the physician. In school systems, we seem to have gone the other way by placing much of the decision-making power in remote places and in the hands of remote persons. It should be possible for all the schools in a large city to be very different, each free to meet the problems of its own area, its own people and its own community.

Along with changes in administrative structure and functioning must come new concepts of what it means to be a teacher and where teaching success is to be found. Studies show that good teachers cannot be identified in terms of their college scholarship. Since teaching is an art, the artist is the all-important factor in the outcome. This is true in all the arts. Research in the area indicates that the most important elements in the teacher's success are his view of himself and his view of other people. These findings in no way minimize the need for knowledge. They do indicate that knowledge alone is inadequate. They do say very definite things to teacher educators as to the kinds of people they should strive to become, as well as to the attitudes and types of behavior they should cultivate. The teacher must learn how to use himself. He cannot become another person or use another's methods.

EDUCATION II

At the very moment of liftoff there is no sense of movement. Man may have passed his own moment of liftoff into ultimate change. Now we have a sense of voyaging in ways that are stranger than our dreams.

An Astronaut

We are changing so swiftly that we do not know what we are or what we may become.

> *Since Hiroshima we have known that the old man must die, the man of devouring ambition, the consuming man must give way to the new man, the learning man, the man of understanding, the servant of life. The future depends upon our opening of ourselves to the emergence of the servant.*
>
> *We now have a growing awareness of the importance of the person. Each man is a universe penetrated by other universes. The world begins with each of us, and no one knows its end.*
>
> *In this transformation we naturally want the strength and goodness of the old man to survive in the new, but the kind of valor and toughness in the old man may now have to yield to a new valor, the courage to joyful surrender. To accept the fact that we are all closely related to one another, breathing upon one another, touching one another whether we want a touch or not.* [4]

Kelly

Man's all consuming problem in the past century was the mastery of the universe, of nature. Our present education has equipped men for this struggle. It has prepared men to be both avaricious and ambitious. Our urban sprawl and decaying cities give evidence of a technological society in which greedy men with ambition help to perpetuate the squalor, when what is needed are men who act with feeling and understanding.

The Public Schools of the nation have made great strides in education during the last half century. If we think of education as it developed in this

---

[4] Frank K. Kelly, "The Possibilities of Transformation", *Saturday Review*, March 7, 1970, p. 17.

century as Education I, the need for Education II becomes apparent. It has taken a few rather uncertain steps but everyday of its experience opens new vistas of achievement. In this volume the point is made that however well Education I has served man in the past, it will not and cannot give us men of learning and understanding here and now; men who are servants of life that are needed in the age of Mankind II. We have taken a look at the current social scene and our present education, in an effort to find the beginnings of Education II, a new education powerful enough to make the difference between success and failure for a free society. We believe Education II will make new assumptions about learning, about human potential, and about the needs of society. Education II will bring about a new mobilization of human resources. It is total community education.

THE EDUCATION CENTERED COMMUNITY

The most distinguishing mark of the new educational program is its close involvement with the life of the entire community. The richness of its program will reach all the people at convenient times and places with offerings adapted to their interests and needs. The education centered community provides education for all. It not only helps people but it also helps people to help themselves. In the school of such a community and in its varied community life, much of the teaching and leadership comes from the people themselves. In the process of helping others they educate themselves.

In the new education centered community, the community school will be the primary agency of oversight and integration in education. It will not take over the functions and prerogatives of the home, but when the home fails it will seek to strengthen the home so that *it* can do better. The school will work in close cooperation with all agencies that can help. When a child does not get an adequate breakfast in the morning, the school will provide it. It does this because it knows it cannot successfully help a hungry and undernourished child to learn. Simultaneously, the home counselor will work with the home in order that before too long the home can provide not only breakfast but a more sanitary, healthful, and psychologically secure place for the child.

Much is said today about our moral crisis, about the breakdown of the family and the community as moral forces in the lives of people. The breakdown is not a matter of decay of individuals so much as the result of the violent upheavals in our society which result from science and technology. Vast numbers of disadvantaged people flow to the northern cities from the rural south. Our population is highly mobile. People change neighbors frequently. Enduring friendships are hard to form. Even at higher economic levels and in educated circles the overemphasis on science and high specialization in our colleges and universities has left such communities short of ideological leadership. We thus face a condition of "uprootedness" at all levels, even within the educational institutions themselves. Education must help people to overcome and to live with the results of this uprootedness. Education can bring people together. It can teach and illustrate human brotherhood by helping individuals relate to each other in satisfying experiences.

The development of the education centered community is thus not only a challenge to our elementary and high schools but equally to our institutions of higher education. The point is that we can no longer take the educational contributions of homes, schools, churches and communities for granted, but must assist them where necessary and when possible enhance their contribution through the school's program and its facilities. The university must itself recognize the current community vacuum and modify its educational programs not only to prepare community leaders of a professional category, but also to provide a better background of general offerings.

Education *can* meet the expectations of the American people. It *can* help our nation to cope with its crisis, but to do so it must recognize the obsolescence of many of our assumptions and practices. If our educators study carefully what we are learning in the inner city they can see clearly not only the need for change but get many suggestions as to the type of education that is needed. The new education should and will take many forms and exemplify many innovations. Experience thus far in work with the disadvantaged suggests that the needed new education will take advantage of the more recent and higher estimates of human potential, will think first of what is happening to the child's self concept, will recognize an enhanced role for the teacher, will seek a decentralized pattern of administration, and will convert the entire community into an educational enterprise.

The current crisis of education is ample evidence that we have waited too long to bring about the change that is needed. It is possible that failure to move or a move that is made too slowly may change the path of American Freedom. Our nation has been strong because the people have been able to make rapid change and to meet all emergencies. Disaster can be avoided by enlisting the leadership of those who determine educational destiny in discarding outmoded beliefs and practices and adopting the new role for education.

103

CHAPTER VII

PROVIDING EQUALITY OF OPPORTUNITY

MESSAGE ON EDUCATION REFORM

*From President Nixon's 1970 Education
Message, sent to the Congress on March 3.*

RICHARD M. NIXON
The President
of the United States

New Measurements of Achievement

What makes a good school? The old answer was a school that maintained high standards of plant and equipment, that had a reasonable number of children per classroom, whose teachers had good college and often graduate training, that kept up to date with new curriculum developments and was alert to new techniques in instruction. This was a fair enough definition so long as it was assumed that there was a direct connection between these school characteristics and the actual amount of learning that takes place in a school.

Years of educational research, culminating in the Equal Educational Opportunity Survey of 1966, have, however, demonstrated that this direct, uncomplicated relationship does not exist.

Apart from the general public interest in providing teachers an honorable and well paid professional career, there is only one important question to be asked about education: What do the children learn?

Unfortunately, it is simply not possible to make any confident deduction from school characteristics as to what will be happening to the children in any particular school. Fine new buildings alone do not predict high achievement. Pupil-teacher ratios may not make as much difference as we used to think. Expensive equipment may not make as much difference as its salesmen would have us believe.

And yet we know that something does make a difference.

The outcome of schooling—what children learn—is profoundly different for different groups of children and different parts of the country. Although we do not seem to understand just what it is in one school or school system that produces a different outcome from another, one conclusion is inescapable: We do not yet have equal educational opportunity in America.

Providing Equality of Opportunity

INTRODUCTION

The need for authority reflects a . . . distrust of human beings . . . the essential philosophy of democracy . . . tells us to trust a person until he proves himself untrustworthy. The prejudiced person . . . distrusts every person until he proves himself trustworthy.

G. W. Allport

Love must be learned, and learned again and again; there is no end to it. Hate needs no instruction, but waits only to be provoked.

Katherine Anne Porter

No nation has given as much attention to equality of educational opportunity as the United States nor has any nation brought as many years of schooling to the average individual. It is therefore somewhat startling to find American education suddenly becoming concerned about lack of equality, particularly as a result of the widespread finding that it is the poor and disadvantaged who suffer most from this lack of equality of opportunity. Most disturbing of all is the changing interpretation of what constitutes equality of educational opportunity. The past notion has been that two pupils attending the same school had equality of opportunity. To state it abstractly, it was assumed that equality of input meant equal opportunity. Now Coleman and others are taking the position that equality of output rather than the equality of input should be the measure of equality of educational opportunity.[1]

THE COLEMAN VIEW

Acceptance of the idea that equality of output is the measure of equality of opportunity has far-reaching and momentous implications for education. One example is to be found in the whole problem of educational support. The Coleman study shows that Northern children rank higher in school achievement than Southern children, Northern white children rank higher than Southern white children, Northern Blacks rank higher than Southern blacks and white children as a whole rank higher than the total of black children. Coleman is taking the position that real equality of opportunity would mean equal achievement *for the averages* of all these groups.[2] This does not mean that all individuals would be equal but that the average achievement for black children as a whole should be equal to that of white children as a whole.

It is obvious that if equal averages are to be achieved, much more money and much more effort must be expended on some groups of children, (notably the children of the poor) than on other groups. What actually happens in America is just the opposite, the wealthier the children's parents, the more is spent on the children's education; the poorer the parents the less is spent.

EDUCATION AND INCOME

Studies of the relationship between income of parents and children's educational achievement indicate that income is a powerful determinant in school achievement. Patricia Sexton, in *Education and Income*, presents startling evidence concerning the school's failure with children from low income families.

One: All schools with $7,000 income achieved above grade level with one exception in the eighth grade. All below $7,000 income achieved below grade.

Two: Achievement scores go up as income levels go up.

---

[1] James S. Coleman, et al. Equality of Educational Opportunity, Washington: U.S. Government Printing Office, 1966.

[2] *Ibid.*

Three: In the fourth grade the lowest income group achieved at a rate two whole grades below the highest income group. [3]

f Sexton found that disadvantaged (low income children) tend to get the poorest teachers, since tenure teachers try to avoid teaching in the inner city. They also get the poorest school buildings since the inner city is the oldest part of the city and the earlier structures remain.

Since children of low income families have a high dropout rate they get proportionately less of what the nation spends on secondary education. Since so few of inner city children finish high school they obviously show smaller percentages attending college.

Riesman and Jencks report that the lowest twenty per cent of our population in income supplies only about four per cent of the college enrollment in the country. [4]

The relationship between family income and school achievement seems an almost diabolical commentary on the American educational system. This system has prided itself on what it could do for the poor. We now discover well past the two-thirds mark in this century that it is the poor with which the school system is a failure. Under our present system of organization, it appears that children from middle class homes have greater opportunity to move upward. In other words, the type of education provided has less influence than the home environment from which a child enters school. Schools as presently constituted, do not make much difference.

THE MYTH OF THE MELTING POT

The figures cited above will no doubt be startling to many citizens who because of past popular public impressions still believe in the "melting pot" idea. Careful study now reveals that the melting pot never really did melt. What really helped the earlier immigrants to become members of American society was membership in a well-organized culture on the European side of the Atlantic. They brought this culture to the new land. In most cases it stressed the relationships between children and parents. It emphasized the importance of learning. Nowhere is this situation shown more strikingly than with the Jewish population, in which the whole concept of the Book plays so large a role. True, our schools did help the children to some degree

[3] Patricia Cayo Sexton, *Education and Income*, New York: Viking Press, 1964, pp. 26-27.

[4] David Riesman and Christopher Jencks, *The Academic Revolution*.

in acquiring the language, but even here they probably acquired more on the streets and on the playground than in the schoolroom. We probably were able to continue to believe in these myths because we did not bother to look at the places where we failed. Constant attention was called to the rapid increase in high school enrollment and the increasing enrollment in universities. All these increases were indeed phenomenal but such figures take no account of the boys and girls at the other end of the distribution . . . the people who dropped out of school, those who did not attend high school, and others who attended for a year or so but then dropped out. Since we studied the figures covering only our successes, it is not surprising that we failed to take account of our failures.

One of the most handicapped elements in our society today is the segment of pupils that has been the product of disadvantaged homes. Their parents have not been able to provide either economic or emotional support, and the children are often a grade or even more, below the appropriate grade level. Neither have they acquired the skills that effective citizenship demands. Their experiences in the schools have been tainted by failure thereby producing a sense of hostility and rejection. The products of this environment are ill-equipped to cope with the problems present in today's society.

PLACE OF RESIDENCE AND INEQUALITY

The places of birth and residence, as well as economic level also contribute to inequality. Children born in poor communities are likely to have less money spent on their education because the tax base is meager. Being born in the United States is, no doubt fortunate, but such benefits are dependent upon the precise locality in which he is born. The geography of the location is significant. One school district able to attract a large industry will benefit by the increase in taxable property. An adjoining district may experience an increase in school population without any increase in taxable property. The result is that a well-financed district may be adjacent to one that may be classified as disadvantaged. The condition of education inequality becomes readily apparent.

It may be contended that state and federal support for education seeks to offset such inequalities, but experience has shown that state and federal grants often compound the difficulty. Campbell points out that such grants are more likely to be additive in the suburbs than in the large cities:

> *It appears that aid is nearly 100 per cent additive to local tax effort in suburban districts while it is less than this, perhaps around 70 per cent additive, in large, central city districts. The result, therefore, is that increases in state aid to local school districts will not offset any gaps in local educational resource bases unless this difference in how aid acts in city and suburban districts is taken into account. Since the amount of per pupil aid received on the average by suburban districts is greater than received by large city districts and since aid is 100 per cent additive in suburban districts, increases in state aid will widen rather than close the gap in educational expenditures between city and suburb.* [5]

The methods for financing education must be changed. The roles played by State and Federal Governments must be enlarged. The criteria for which grants are made to individual school districts, must be changed.

The share of school support carried by the State and Federal government has been increasing slowly but the trend is strong enough to suggest that there will be a time when the federal government will make sure that no American child will be denied his birthright for a good education. Similarly, states are beginning to assume a larger responsibility. In some states it has been proposed that the entire tax burden of supporting education be taken over by the State. If a child is to be the victim of the poverty of the area immediately around the house in which he lives, it is inevitable that the poor will continue to suffer disadvantage. Minimum support levels for education for all American children must be established. State and Federal governments must play larger roles in the establishment of minimum levels. When more adequate funds for education are provided, a question will arise concerning the distribution of these funds among school districts. At the present time, rich districts get the full benefits of their wealth and the poor districts still suffer from the impact of their poverty. If this situation is to be corrected, the principle must be established that the distribution of financial sources in education must be determined by the needs of the area and the needs of the children involved. This would mean that a school district with a large proportion of low economic level homes would receive a larger share of the tax monies available than would a wealthy district. Such an arrangement would take into account the complex educational problems that are associated with schools in low income areas.

---

[5] Alan K. Campbell, "Who Governs the Schools", *Saturday Review*, December 21, 1968, pp. 50-52, 63-65.

If it is proposed that such a policy would fly in the face of traditional practice, it can only be stated that the public must be helped to understand the crucial character of this problem. One of the public relations tasks of professional educators in the next decade is to bring the crucial character of this problem of educational disadvantage to the attention of people in all areas and at all levels of economic position or leadership.

COMPLEXITY OF THE PROBLEM OF EDUCATIONAL INEQUALITY

In the last ten years there has been much experimentation with compensatory education. Dropouts have been brought back to school for what is more or less the repetition of their earlier work. Special programs have been instituted in many places and efforts are made to measure such programs, the results of which are often disappointing. We have a chance to explain these disappointing results when we take a look at the complexity of the problem of inequality of opportunity. No doubt, this is a reflection of the general social, economic and cultural conditions of the community. If children are attending a school in which the economic, cultural and social level is high, we may assume that the impact of the homes and the rest of the community is favorable to the success of the school's efforts. In a community where the parents are very poor, and without education, in which the community conditions are inadequate, it may be assumed that such conditions operate to the disadvantage of the school and its program. Consequently, it is a mistake to assume that some small alteration in the teaching method, in curriculum or any other area of the school life will in and of itself alter the current situation. This is not to say that such changes in curriculum, methodology and general school conditions are not desirable. It is to say that such changes within the schoolhouse itself cannot be expected to change the achievements of the children when the supporting conditions necessary for good school achievement are absent in home and community.

For many decades school people have tried hard to develop interest on the part of the public in our schools. The Parent-Teacher Association, school programs, public relation organizations and many other devices have made efforts to interest the public. None of these efforts has been unduly successful. Probably the reason is that in virtually all of them the public has sensed that it was on the receiving end. It was being educated, informed, and sometimes brain-washed by professional people. Citizens have not felt that they were contributors to education but rather that they were asked to assume financial responsibility and give carte blanche backing to professional people. In all of this, they sensed a feeling of inferiority in comparison with the professional teacher.

If one suggests that a citizen ought to take a course, the suggestion implies that he needs further education. This may be something of a blow to his ego and may account for the difficulty in persuading many people to take part in adult education. If the same person is invited to the school to assist in a program for children and youth, it becomes a compliment to his ego and his self-image is improved. Experiences in recent years in community schools bear out this point in striking ways. Through community school experience in various parts of the country, countless hundreds of parents and citizens have become involved and in the process built their own interests in further education as well as developed a better self-image and a better understanding of education generally.

One of the important reasons we, as educators, have failed to develop the maximum potential of most children is because we have placed so little emphasis on education of the community. Most citizens are unaware of the goals, plans, and aspirations of schools for the development of individual potential. A majority of lay citizens in the community know little about the school function, its instructional program and its problems.

The impact of this lack of awareness and involvement is shattering. It is especially devastating to an institution whose very existence is dependent upon community support. As an illustration, one would never attempt to approach an individual with an item bearing a three to five hundred dollar price tag and ask that he purchase it sight unseen. The example may be a bit overdrawn, however, our educational millage and bond issues are often requests for support of an unseen product. At best, our client knowledge of the package is only superficial. The above illustration suggests why, in so many instances, the answer to our requests for school support has often been a "no"!

> *The traveler's eye-view of men and women is not satisfying. A man might spend his life in trains and restaurants and know nothing of humanity at the end. To know, one must be an actor as well as a spectator.*
> Aldous Huxley

The fact that we have failed to inform the public becomes especially significant when we come to deal with the problem of equality of opportunity in education. Here we are confronting the demands of a new society, which cannot be met without the fullest knowledge on the part of our people as to the nature of the problems we face and the programs that will be required.

113

THE CRUCIAL NEED FOR A NEW EQUALITY

In modern industrial society, no one can contribute effectively nor enjoy the full blessing of freedom unless his education has made it possible for him to do so. In other words in our kind of society education of all of the people is imperative. We cannot condone or accept failure. All must be educated. If all are to be educated, inequality of opportunity cannot be tolerated.

It is at this point that community education becomes a tremendous force in the solution of the problem of educational inequality of opportunity. Community education, properly interpreted, mobilizes all of the resources of the community and places them at the disposal of all of the people of the community including the children and their parents. With this type of educational mobilization, it is possible to undertake the education of each child and adult making sure that no stone is unturned to give each individual the opportunity for his fullest development. This goal cannot be met by schools staffed by traditional teachers, offering outdated curriculum, and kept open from nine in the morning until three in the afternoon. A completely mobilized community does have the resources to accomplish what is so imperative in our present society. Communities thus organized would provide facilities and finance to the extent that the total community could accept its responsibilities to all individuals and groups.

It should be remembered that total community education is not a gimmick, a cure-all, or some mystical device that will revolutionize education overnight. It is a plan for education of children, parents, and all of the people of the community. It is conducted in such a way that it not only provides all the people of a community and their children with the education they need but also reveals their additional educational and social needs from time to time. Such education helps people to undertake community ventures designed to improve the quality of living in the community. It helps people to help themselves. It mobilizes the people of the community for effective action in getting better support for education, in improving the physical conditions of the community such as housing, streets, recreational facilities and police protection.

It is important to stress that community education is not an extra program that is attached to the existing curriculum. It is not "frosting on the cake". It is the cake! It is a marble cake that includes all segments of the community, around the clock — twelve months a year. It is a new dimension that provides unlimited educational opportunities.

If such a community really studies its educational problems, it will conclude that the true meaning of educational equality is made up of educational output rather than input in money and human effort. In other words: Is there equality in what large groups of children in the community are able to accomplish through the process of education? A community can decide that the achievements of the poor should equal the achievements of the children of the rich. A community can decide that the achievements of black children will equal the achievements of white children. In such an environment, the community effort recognizes the worth of human potential and the development of the self-image for each individual. The result is a new appreciation and a collective interest in human betterment. This can be accomplished by an effective program of community education. The elimination of inequality of educational opportunity must be attacked on every front. There is no panacea that can be a cure-all. Team teaching, educational television, teaching machines and the like are useful devices, but they alone are not sufficient. The program must concern itself with the total life of the child, the total life of the school and the total life of the community. Every stone must be turned.

CHAPTER VIII

ONE SOCIETY OR TWO?

One Society or Two?

INTRODUCTION

More than a hundred years after the liberation of slaves, our society is becoming keenly aware of the problems that have their roots in a combination of racial, economic and educational injustice. Even those who have faced what Gunnar Myrdal called "An American Dilemma" often have only an intellectual awareness of the depth of the problem. As a result, we become the easy victims of the oversimplifiers and are often misled by a faulty study of our history as a people.

The melting pot concept, based on a faith in gradualism supported by education, has dominated our thinking and has especially influenced the educational profession. Accuse the average educator of being a racist and you insult him. He is also hurt because he is conscious of no prejudice. He can even show that he has worked for desegregation and strongly favored equal educational opportunity for all regardless of color or economic status. Other national groups "made it" in America through education. Give us time and the black man will "make it" in the same way.

Running through all of this is the popular belief that the public school is the escalator whereby the child from a poverty-stricken home can rise to a high position in society. The myth of the school as an escalator lives on.

119

It lives on because in relatively rare instances it happens. There are poor who rise to high levels, so the assumption is that if others do not "make it" the fault is their own. We know now that those who "make it" are the rare exceptions. We are learning that the school is, for large numbers of the poor, a stark tragedy. Large proportions of the black people are poor. They therefore did not have equal opportunity. The whole issue of what constitutes equal opportunity in education is treated elsewhere in this volume.

At this point it is emphasized that under past concepts of equal educational opportunity, the black child is a sufferer not only of the results of racial discrimination, but also from a fallacious concept of what is meant by equality of opportunity. The latter he shares with the poor white child and the poor child of any minority group.

BLACK SEPARATISM

The slow pace of desegregation together with the continued flight of the middle class to the suburbs has discouraged many black people, leading some of them to despair of ever achieving significant integration. Such despairing persons often opt for complete separation through the establishment of a separate black society. While the proportion of our Negro people who favor such separation is as yet not large, the separatist leadership is militant and vigorous. Unless real improvement takes place rapidly in the general acceptance of black people in our society, extremists favoring a separate black society can be expected to have a larger audience.

To the vast majority of Americans the mere thought of a separate black society is abhorrent. It is especially repugnant to the educational profession in human terms and if carried out, it would spell defeat for the educator's most cherished dream of making mankind the master of its own destiny through education. If we cannot through education become one people regardless of color, then we must of necessity scale down our hope for human gains through education and accept lower expectations and diminished hopes for humanity in general.

The issue of black separatism must be viewed not only in terms of the effect of separation on the black population but also in terms of the impact on the white people. Tragic and injurious as racial prejudice has been in its impact on the black people, its legacy for the white people is equally or more damaging. Here we must remember that human beings grow in the degree that they accept their brotherhood with all men. If I discriminate against a man because of his color, I hurt him but I inflict a greater injury upon myself.

I narrow my own spirit. I become something less as a person. Meanness and smallness take the place of largeness and generosity in my personality. As this process occurs with others as with myself the whole white society is narrowed, embittered, becoming a small society instead of a great society. Since the black man shares this attitude of rejection toward white people, he too is reduced in stature. The result is that we all become something less than we could be if only we could accept all human beings.

Seen entirely from the point of view of our black people, it seems that little but permanent inferiority can result from such a separation. It would, of course, play directly into the hands of those elements in the population that are racist in attitude; elements which have fought school desegregation and nearly all progress in civil rights. Moreover, the separatist movement has placed the sincere hard working white people who have worked for racial equality in a confused position, even though they have done all they could through education and community activities to build one society rather than two.

THE DEMAND FOR COMMUNITY CONTROL

The failure of the educational establishment to serve the educational needs of the children of the poor has been documented. This failure falls with special severity on the children of black citizens. So incensed have many of our black people become over this failure that in many Inner City areas they are demanding what amounts to almost complete control over the education that their children are to receive. They believe that our present school systems, controlled as they see it by a white educational establishment, have no real intention of educating their children for a life of equality with other Americans. Many blacks are so discouraged over the slow progress of the effort toward integration that many of them believe it to be a hopeless cause and that the only solution in providing equality of educational opportunity lies in schools that are controlled and taught by blacks for the children of black people. Preston Wilcox says it this way:

> The incarceration of black people behind the "colored curtain" and the failure of "good intentions" to lead poor Blacks anywhere but toward hell has provided the evidence around which black Americans have begun to organize. It is up to black people to remove white profit from black ghettos, to assume leadership of institutions serving the black community. To develop and advocate system for Blacks and to develop the political strength of its social fabric, is the ultimate challenge facing black Americans. Interestingly enough the integration of essentially white institutions

will arise less from the expression of social commitment by whites than by pressure from the black community.

The shift in group interests is occurring on several levels.

1. *From a one by one approach (i.e. Jackie Robinson and Kenneth Clark) to efforts enmasse.*

2. *From an appeal to white conscience, to an appeal to black consciousness.*

3. *From reliance on white leadership to the exercise of effective black leadership.*

4. *From excessive identification with the values of the white oppressor to a redefinition of these values appropriate to the aspirations of black people.*

5. *From entrapment as economic consumers to an elaboration of roles as economic producers.*

6. *From political dependence to political independence.*

7. *From the role of victimized plaintiff to that of articulate participation - proponent of specific changes to benefit Blacks directly.*[1]

Some black leaders believe that schools for black children controlled by black people themselves will provide a radically different education than that now received in most cities. The authors doubt that black control can so radically change the schools. Black children suffer from built-in weaknesses of the school system which operate on all children regardless of color. The authors believe that a new program of education must be developed which will give equality of opportunity to all children regardless of color or economic status.

The question really becomes: Are black children really suffering because their schools are controlled by white people or are they suffering because of innate, built-in weaknesses of the schools which will militate against them no matter who controls the operation. The authors hold that the methodologies, the curricula, and the whole establishment operates against the fullest development of the children of the poor, black and white.

[1] Robert L. Green, *Racial Crisis in American Education,* Chicago: The Follett Educational Corporation, 1969, p. 311.

Even if we had no black people in America, even if all our people were white and middle class, the authors believe that decentralization and some measure of community involvement are urgently necessary at the present moment. The real question is not whether there should be community control or no community control but rather about the process whereby the community can participate in the education of its own children. Already, there are people who see in our early experimentation in community control evidence that the wrong kind of arrangements for community control may exercise a divisive effect on our communities and militate against integration leading to two Americas rather than one. Irving Kritol writing in The Public Interest makes the following statement:

> *What New York's black militants really want, what they are competing with one another for, is not the overthrow of the white "establishment" but sovereignty over the black populace. And this the Whites are, in the end, likely to be only too willing to grant them.*
>
> *This is what lies behind the whole "decentralization" issue in New York and that is why the related topic of "community control" is so crucial. The question of depriving white ethnic groups of their present positions — as teachers, sanitationmen, policemen, firemen, construction workers, etc. — for the presumed benefit of Blacks is inflammatory, as it is intended to be. But that is not the ultimate meaning of this controversy. (The Blacks are already moving into these jobs in a massive way, and in some cases now are "represented" beyond their proportion of the population.) What is ultimate is — well, to see that, let us assume that "community control" has been effected, and then let us imagine what New York City is like. There will be black communities having control over their own services, over all the jobs in the area, over their own local budget, over housing, etc. Next to them, there will be white communities with comparable powers. And now let us ask: how does a man move from one to the other? The answer is short and easy; he won't be able to. And this, precisely, is what the militant black nationalists are after.*
>
> *A shifting power base makes power hungry men anxious and insecure. And it is for this reason that the black nationalists have, with great political acumen, raised the matter of "community control". They want to freeze the neighborhoods of New York. They want to prevent middle class or working class Blacks from moving to the white areas, elsewhere in the city or in the suburbs. Their aim is apartheid, because only in apartheid can they ensure their rule. Nor do they care about the economic and social consequences. The poorer, the more ignorant, the*

123

more isolated the black communities are the better the chances for black nationalist leaders to play upon their grievances and to stimulate their fantasies.

Lower middle income Whites in or near the gray areas who live in fear and resentment of Negroes and the ghetto, would like nothing better than to have the power to keep Negroes out and to maintain "their" neighborhoods. Thus, the great diversity of New York's population and the inevitable tensions among its groups lend decentralization an almost universal appeal; to each group and neighborhood it promises power, status, territorial integrity, and an immunity from threatening others.[2]

It seems clear that the development described by Kristol can not be the answer. Citizens, whether black or white, must accept responsibility for providing a school system that will give priority to the needs of children and youth wherever they are. Recent developments point to the advantages of biracial school experience. Effort must be expended to see that those who direct the school enterprise have a commitment to the best practices in school administration. When research has demonstrated the validity of practice, that knowledge should be used for improving the educational opportunities for all. If this can become inherent in our guidelines for change, the separatist movement will be dissipated.

The key concern here is the preservation of one America, a self repairing society that is in process of unification and that allows for diversity. The Community Education concept has come of age. For many it has become a slogan . . . a slogan too often without meaning. To others it represents a view that destroys the establishment. The viewpoint posits community education as complete community control . . the complete breakdown of any unity . . . a move toward diversity . . . the balkanization of the American school systems. To this school of thought Community Education implies complete neighborhood or community control. Thus it could be a movement toward fragmentation, isolation, diversity, duplication, discontinuity and in many cases divisiveness, all of which are the antithesis of the type of community mobilization through community education the authors envision. The history of developing any semblance of unity out of a system based on divisiveness is dismal.

---

[2] Irving Kristol, "Who Knows New York", *The Public Interest*. Summer Issue, 1969.

The community education envisioned in this volume works to bring people and agencies together, rather than to further the ghettoization of any citizen. It is a search for a new unity that allows for diversity.

AN EDUCATION FOR ONE SOCIETY

If we accept the concept of one society, a great responsibility must be accepted by education. Present education fails signally to build a good self-concept on the part of the poor. We have been exceedingly slow to recognize the role played by the individual's self-concept. As a result, we do not see that much of our school practice is destructive to the child's view of himself. While such practices affect all children, they fall with special brutality upon the minority child whose feelings of alienation in society adds to the feelings of inferiority inherent in many of our educational practices such as the marking system and ability grouping.

The proportion of poor among black people is higher, nearly 50 per cent higher. Beyond this, the black child bears the burden of the whole society's discriminatory practices. If we turn to the massive Coleman study we see the situation in greater detail. Here is a resume of the findings:

1. The great importance of family background for achievement;

2. The fact that the relation of family background to achievement does not diminish over the years of school;

3. The relatively small amount of school-to-school variation that is not accounted for by difference in family background, indicating the small independent effect of variations in school facilities, curriculum and staff upon achievement;

4. The small amount of variance in achievement explicitly accounted for by variations in facilities and curriculum;

5. Given the fact that no school factors account for much variation in achievement, teachers' characteristics account for more than any other—taken together with the results from (the section on characteristics of staff), which show that teachers tend to be socially and racially similar to the students they teach;

6. The fact that the social composition of the student body is more highly related to achievement, independently of the student's own social background, than is any school factor;

125

7. The fact that attitudes such as a sense of control of the environment, are extremely highly related to achievement, but appear to be little influenced by variation in school characteristics.

Taking all these results together, one implication stands out above all: That schools bring little influence to bear on a child's achievement that is independent of his background and general social context; and that this very lack of an independent effect means that the inequalities imposed on children by their home, neighborhood, and peer environment are carried along to become the inequalities with which they confront adult life at the end of school. For equality of educational opportunity through the schools must imply a strong effect of schools that is independent of the child's immediate social environment, and that strong independent effect is not present in American schools. [3]

Here we confront again the most baffling characteristic of current education in America. Differences in schools as they now exist account for little in differences in achievement. Differences in home and community background are, by comparison, powerful in their effect on the child's achievement. Thus, there is little reason to believe that even the best improvements we can visualize will do little to give equal opportunity to the poor, to the poor black children, unless an entirely different concept of education is developed. This different concept must come to grips with the problem of improving the home and the community. The school must educate the people of the community, the parents. It must involve the parents in their own education and the education of their own people.

Seen in terms of the educational developments of the past decade, Coleman's study is most disturbing. The bulk of effort to improve education in the last decade has gone into school-centered areas. Increased educational technology, television, audio-visual aids, flexible scheduling, teaching machines and team teaching, all may be useful in the right place, but all are *schoolhouse* linked. It is questionable that if all were used and used well they would make a great difference in the education of the ghetto child. This is not to say that these and other devices would not improve ghetto education if the two powerful factors in achievement were altered, namely, the characteristics of the teachers and changes made in the child's total environment.

[3] Clement Vose, "School Desegregation: A Political Scientist's View", *Affirmative School Integration: Efforts to Overcome DeFacto Segregation in Urban Schools*. Beverly Hills, California: Sage Publications, 1967-1968, pp. 143-144.

A DUAL TASK

While the ineffectiveness of our current educational programs have contributed heavily to the present plight of black people in our society, it is nevertheless true that thousands of teachers and educational leaders have struggled faithfully to overcome these handicaps and to bring about an end to segregation and discrimination. Unfortunately, many of these efforts seem actually to have backfired. For example, when the percentage of black people in a school reaches a certain point the tendency is for the white people to move out bringing about a further concentration of black children and actually resegregating the population. The most striking example of this is Washington, D. C. where now, more than ninety per cent of the pupils in the public school are black. In many northern cities, housing patterns have concentrated the black citizens in ghetto areas. The problem of desegregation cannot be solved without transportation of children or a revolution in the housing patterns. Poor people live where they live because it is the only place they can afford to live. They cannot move unless their incomes can be increased. Their incomes will not increase unless they are given new saleable skills. The fact is that the majority of the white middle class population in our country simply does not realize the crucial character of the problem. There is another instance in which our education has failed.

Education thus faces a double problem in relation to the task of creating one rather than two societies. In the first place, we face the problem of carrying on an educational program which provides all the equality of opportunity possible under the current conditions. In the second place, we have the responsibility for changing public attitudes in such directions that the total environment in which the educational program is carried on is changed. No one can read the United States Riot Commission Report entitled "The Report of the National Advisory Commission on Civil Disorders" without reaching the conclusion that we in America will either solve our racial problems by bringing full justice to black and other minority groups or our society will not continue to be the free country it has been. The steps which are necessary to bring about greater equality of educational opportunity are not palatable to many people, but the price of our failure to do so will be a fragmented society and one in which freedom will not flourish.

CHAPTER IX

LEADERSHIP IN PROFESSIONAL GROWTH

Leadership In Professional Growth

INTRODUCTION

Few areas are more full of controversy than that of teacher education. The controversy is nowhere more heated than inside the universities with their constant differences over the relative importance of subject matter knowledge and professional skills and insights. No other profession has found the recognition of professionalization so difficult to achieve. No one even in the sciences, doubts the need for "learning by doing" in the education of the doctor, but the same scientist may scoff at courses in education and deny that the teacher needs to know anything about children and their growth and development. The result of all the controversy has been to retard teacher education, discourage innovation and darken the teacher's own view of his professional preparation.

PHYSICIAN, HEAL THYSELF!

In no case has the weakness of teacher preparation become more evident than in the inner city, and in other schools enrolling disadvantaged children. Such children bear the special brunt of the teacher's lack of competence and especially the absence of the personal qualities that would enable the teacher to deal effectively with disadvantaged children. In other words, the disadvantaged setting subjects the entire educational structure to very severe tests, so severe that the system fails and in the failure its anatomy becomes visible.

What we are witnessing in many urban schools today is demonstration of the fallacy of an educational theory which holds that there is extant a body of subject matter the mastery of which constitutes an education. It is true that disadvantaged children are failing to learn subject matter but they are failing for the very reason that the school tries to inject this subject matter into the life of the child . . . a life which is hostile to the material and the culture of which it is a part. Inner city children like all others have proved that they can learn before they enter school. They have learned one of the most complex things human beings learn, namely a language. They have learned this language not in classes but in the totality of their living in home and community. This learning can be successfully continued but not the way schools do it. Such children can continue to learn successfully if education comes to grips with their whole environment and if teachers understand children and know the conditions necessary for their learning. Thus, we can see that our confrontation of disadvantaged, especially in the inner city is saying something to us about our teacher preparation. What it is saying is that education is more than learning facts and acquiring skills. It is the process of becoming and accordingly, what a teacher is, takes precedence over what he knows.

The child is suffering from the defects of the education that he is experiencing and his teacher is handicapped by having received an education having the same defects. Thus, the reform of teacher education is really the reform of all education. This is true because our most persistent educational problems arise from the central fallacy of all schools, namely, that education consists of acquiring information rather than a process of becoming.

Inner city parents are extremely critical of the teachers, believing them to be prejudiced against the children for racial and/or social class reasons. This may be true in some cases. A greater reason for the failure of inner-city children comes not from racial or social prejudice but from a misconception of educational priorities and a lack of the personal qualities and behavior on the part of many teachers. This deficiency prevents the development of a favorable environment for learning and a positive self image. Even if all our children were of one color and of one economic and social class our education and our teachers would not escape the trap they are in because children would still suffer from an education that emphasizes the wrong goals.

Black children face discrimination and injustice not only because they are black, but also because they suffer from schoolhouse isolation, a built-in weakness which all children face. In such a setting the emphasis is upon cognitive learning and our traditional belief that education consists solely of gaining knowledge and developing skills. Black parents and children would be surprised how little of their present school difficulty would disappear were they suddenly white. They would find that their poverty combined with the educational fallacies of the teachers and schools account for most of their difficulty. Racial prejudice is a factor but only one element. Even if we could eliminate such prejudice overnight our most persistent educational problems would still remain.

One cannot spend years in schools and colleges without sensing that there is something deadly about school . . . about the academic climate. Why is it that children in the first grade show curiosity, spontaneity and happiness, yet in a few years they are apathetic, withdrawn and bored? John Holt says it this way:

> *Nobody starts off stupid. You have only to watch babies and infants, and think seriously about what all of them learn and do to see that except for the most grossly retarded, they show a style of life, and a desire and ability to learn that in an older person we might call genius. Hardly an adult in a thousand, or ten thousand could in any three years of his life learn as much, grow as much in his understanding of the world around him, as every infant learns and grows in his first three years. But what happens as we get older to this extraordinary capacity for learning and intellectual growth?*

> *What happens is that it is destroyed and more than by any other one thing, by the process that we misname education, a process that goes on in most homes and schools. We adults destroy most of the intellectual and creative capacity of children by the things we do to them or make them do. We destroy this capacity above all by making them afraid, afraid of not doing what other people want, of not pleasing, of making mistakes, of failing, of being wrong.*

> *We destroy the disinterested, (we do not mean uninterested) love of learning in children, which is strong when they are small, by encouraging and compelling them to work for petty and contemptible rewards . . . we kill not only their curiosity, but their feeling that it is good and an admirable thing to be curious . . .*[1]

---

[1] John Holt, *How Children Fail* (New York: Dell Publishing Co., Inc. 1964), pp. 167-168.

It is evident that the present climate for education must be changed. What is needed is an educational experience that will further the child's effort to become a human being worthy of confidence and self respect. He will be motivated to develop his intellectual and creative capacity in positive ways.

THE ART OF TEACHING

Combs'[2] research in teacher education gives scant support for the conventional patterns of teacher education. He finds that no small part of our problem in teacher education grows out of the persistent tendency to see teaching as a technical field in which methods and activities can be determined without regard to the person who uses them. Teaching is not a science. It is an art and in the arts the artist is the all important consideration. No scientific combination of colors will make a great painting. Painting is an art, and one becomes an artist by working at the art. This is the essence of the arts. They are personal . . . a committee, however accomplished, cannot produce a great painting; only an individual can. The artist in turn uses the tools of science, particularly those found in the behavioral sciences.

Combs insists that each teacher must learn how to use himself, he cannot copy others however accomplished they may be. If each teacher must use himself, then the challenge in teacher education is to produce teachers who are self-actualizing persons, who being self-actualizing people can help children to become self-actualizing persons.

Most of our present education stops the growth toward self-actualization. We are the products of an environment that has made our actualization the work of others not that of ourselves. Most of our academic learning has been assigned, controlled and evaluated by others. Purposeful learning is not mastered in this way. We do not learn to manage our own learning activities. We do not really find out what we think and believe. We have been too busy memorizing what others think.

---

[2] Arthur W. Combs, (ed) *Perceiving, Behaving, Becoming.* (Washington, D.C.: Yearbook, Association for Supervision and Curriculum Development, National Education Association, 1962.)

Our unique qualities, insights and understandings are not developed. We don't find out who we are. Unless we know who we are, what kind of people we are, how can we learn how to use ourselves?[3] One cannot use effectively what he does not know or understand.

HOW KIDS LEARN STUFF

A seven year old child once assured John M. Culkin S J.[4] that education is: "How Kids Learn Stuff." Children often have a way of bringing an eloquent simplicity to what adults have made artificially complex. Education is the process of "kids learning stuff" and teaching is the process of facilitating that learning. If we were to analyze the above definition we could conclude with John Culkin that teachers generally know their "stuff." The "stuff" in this case is a body of knowledge that revolves around a subject matter or content field. However, teachers seem to know little about learning and even less about the children (kids) they teach.

Professional educational preparation, therefore, must strive to provide a balance in the three broad areas of *content, learning theory*, and *child psychology*, which will of necessity give teacher preparation an interdisciplinary nature.

First, professional preparation must be concerned with the development of a body of subject matter. Teacher preparation must seek to provide excellence in the specific *content areas* that facilitate skills in communications, human relations, aesthetics and the skills required by a modern technology.

Secondly, professional preparation must concern itself with knowledge of the *learning process* and *learning theory*. The "seat of the pants" teacher is an anachronism. It is as much of an anachronism as the "seat of the pants" pilot, doctor or scientist. Teachers must know and use the scientific knowledge that has been amassed on *how, when, why, where* and *what* individuals learn. The masterful, timely and wise use of this scientific evidence is the true art of teaching.

---

[3] Arthur T. Jersild, *When Teachers Face Themselves.* (New York: Teachers College Press, Columbia University, 1955.

[4] John M. Culkin, S. J., "A Schoolman's Guide to Marshall McLuhan," *Saturday Review*, March 18, 1967.

Thirdly and closely related to the above two, is a need for an understanding of the individual learner. It is in this area that professional preparation is failing. A search for this understanding begins within the teacher, and through studies in content fields that include psychology, sociology, anthropology and other areas of human behavior.

The true professional maintains a balance, a perspective, an equilibrium between knowledge of content (subject matter) learning motivational and instructional theory, and an understanding of the learner. Paraphrasing Robert R. Blake and Jane S. Mouton[5], we need professionals who are 10-10-10 based on a scale of 1-10 for each of the three above areas that constitute true artistry and balance in teaching. Too often teachers have operated in a 10-1-1 fashion. Content is emphasized to the exclusion of an awareness of the learning process and the needs, perceptions and expectations of the client, the student.

There is at least one other basic idea that must be considered in the professional preparation of educators. It is an awareness of the impact of change and the tempo of a dynamic, protean society. The explosion of knowledge in all three areas listed above which constitute professional preparation, and the challenges of these changes demand that a professional education be aware of the dynamism of our society — a stance that implies constant movement, self-evaluation, personal and professional growth.

It is becoming increasingly apparent that what a teacher or educational leader *is* has as much impact on his effectiveness as what he knows. Is there a profile of characteristics that reveal those who possess qualities and attributes that make them effective as teachers and leaders? More importantly, if these characteristics can be identified, can professional preparation influence the development of productive personal characteristics? There is evidence that the answer to both of the above questions is an emphatic yes!

What attributes then, characterize the successful educational leader, the successful community educator? The authors posit the following profile for leadership in education.

---

[5]   Blake and Mouton. *The Managerial Grid*, Gulf Publishing Co.: Houston, Texas, 1964.

PROFILE OF AN EDUCATIONAL LEADER

Ten characteristics of people who possess leadership abilities:

1. They have vision: They are aware of what's happening around them. They have long antennae, and are very receptive and open to new ideas. They are aware of what people need. They see the world in terms of what it might become, rather than in the way it is. "They have their eyes on the stars and their feet on the ground." They are constantly searching for a better way, a different way, avoiding the "Calf Paths" of the mind, the routines that trap man's creativeness.

2. They have faith in peoples' ability to grow. They have a high estimate of human potential. They believe in all kinds of people. They have a high tolerance for ambiguity. They respect and encourage uniqueness in the individual. They have plus-plus personalities. They believe in themselves, and they have faith in others. They operate with a belief that "I can and so can you." Thomas Harris,[6] M.D. refers to it as a life position that responds to the world with "I'm OK - You're OK" behavior.

In contrast to the plus-plus, "I'm OK - You're OK" life position we find others that manifest a plus-minus, or "I'm OK - You're not OK" life style. An authoritarian, close-minded "If you want it done right do it yourself" stance.

In others a position of personal despair and hopelessness is manifested through a minus-plus or "I'm not OK - You're OK" style of behavior.

The final and most devastating posture is the minus-minus or "I'm not OK - You're not OK" view of reality. Manifesting itself in complete despair in self and society. Often it is a rationalization for personal inadequacies and a projection of these inadequacies to others and to society in general.

The plus-plus, "I'm OK - You're OK" personality sees people not only as they are but in terms of what they might become. They sense the potential in man. Goethe said "Treat a man as he is, you diminish him, treat him as he may become, you enoble him". The great teachers

---

[6] Thomas Harris, I'm OK — You're OK, Harper & Row, N. Y. 1969.

of history have taught to the man or adult in the child overlooking present immaturities in developing tomorrow's men.

3. They are optimistic. They see the world as if it were the morning, not the evening. They are seldom pessimistic or defeatist. They believe in the ultimate triumph of the human spirit. The story may be apocryphal, but Howard Hughes is reported to have given *Trans World Airlines* its name when it was a one pilot - one plane operation. The genius of the future is that man invents most of it. The degree to which this is true increases the impact of optimism and hope for a better tomorrow.

4. They make a gift of themselves. They are involved. They are not indifferent to the needs of society. They are dedicated to goals of education and give of themselves freely to achieve these goals. They believe in what they are doing and what we are doing. They strive for excellence.

5. They are imaginative. They draw heavily on their own imagination and on the imagination of others. They refuse to be complacent. They never feel that they have "arrived". What they do today reminds them of what must be done tomorrow. The solution of one problem generates ideas for solution to other problems.

6. They are good listeners. They have the ability to read people. They have empathy and reciprocity. They are perceptive people. There is an old adage: "God gave us two ears and one mouth and he intended that they be used in that proportion."

7. They are not jealous people. They surround themselves with capable people. They enjoy other's achievements. They bask in reflective glory, enjoying their part in the success of others.

8. They are accessible. They have time for people. They don't hide behind desks, secretaries, and formalities. They are aware of non-verbal communications - *The Silent Language.* [7]

---

[7]   Edward Hall, *The Silent Language*, Fawcett Publications, Greenwich, Conn. 1969.

9. They are more interested in *what* is right rather than *who* is right. They are open-minded. [8]

10. They are secure people. They are not easily threatened. They are not egg-walkers. They are not marionettes. They have convictions and the courage to express and work for these convictions.

And finally, they are "Theory Y people" not "Theory X people". [9] Theory X people see man as willfully lazy, capricious, and in need of constant watching. Theory Y people on the other hand believe that man is responsible and capable of self-control. McGregor suggests that Theory Y assumptions correspond more nearly to evidence derived from research into human capability. Theory X represents a traditional view of direction and control based on striving for task achievement only, with no real consideration or recognition of the importance of individual needs for self-development, inclusion, and affection. Theory Y individuals search for a balance, a perspective, an equilibrium between two purposes of any human endeavor! (1) accomplishment of the task and (2) consideration of the individual needs, motives, values and attitudes of the participants.

Theory Y people, therefore, are those who sense a need to accomplish a task, but also sense the need to maintain humanistic and humanitarian principles in perspective while striving for the task. A Theory Y person would, therefore, not destroy a child's faith in himself, smash an ego, destroy a self image in the name of accomplishing a task, such as teaching the child to read even if it meant destroying the child or his love for school or reading in the process. An individual that conducts his affairs in a Theory X manner might have few compulsions as he destroys an individual's imagination, ingenuity and creativity in a single-minded quest to accomplish the prescribed task. One only has to think of the inhumanities heaped on man in misguided efforts to teach the humanities, to sense the devastating impact of a Theory X philosophy upon the educational process.

The new type of education envisioned will require a new educator, new administrator and new approaches to preparation of both. The problems we face in education are cyclical. History has taught us the best way to attack a cyclical problem is at all points on the cycle. We must pull out all the stops.

---

[8] Milton Rokeach, *Open and Closed Mind,* Basic Books, New York, 1960

[9] Douglas McGregor, *The Human Side of Enterprise,* 1960

We must also start somewhere. A new education must begin with a new type of preparation. We cannot expect teachers and administrators to be concerned with the affective considerations of the educational process if only the cognitive concerns are emphasized and practiced in the preparation of their programs.

What we speak of in this volume as total community education is an integrated whole. We need a new education which stimulates curiosity, develops eagerness instead of boredom, happiness for learners instead of frustration. To get such education we must have teachers with goals, methods and attitudes which produce the climate for learning. A school which destroys curiosity in children will probably do the same for adults. It is not merely the lighted schoolhouse in the evening, not only extending education to all the people of the community, but good education for all . . . children and adults alike. To produce this kind of education we must have teachers who believe in it and who in personality and competence are equipped to provide it. Education II will not be static, it will be characterized by dynamism and growth. To insure such dynamism administrative organization and leadership must be consistent with the new education.

CHAPTER X

**LIBERATING PRINCIPALS, TEACHERS,
PARENTS AND CHILDREN**

Liberating Principals, Teachers, Parents and Children

INTRODUCTION

Few people outside of the educational establishment itself probably realize how restrictive the bureaucratic administrative establishment has become. The chain of command has become long with level after level of administrators whose approval must be secured before certain kinds of changes can be instituted. Thus, the problem is not only to change the points of view and practices of teachers but permission must be secured to translate these points of view and practices into reality. In a large school system this process is so long and time-consuming that often those who propose changes become completely frustrated and go on to other things before permission is secured. This frustration is felt not only by teachers but by principals, by middle management; and even by parents and citizens in the community. Often Board Members hesitate to propose changes realizing full well how difficult the process will be to carry a proposal to the manifold administrative levels.

While the frustration occasioned by the bureaucracy can be disruptive in any kind of educational organization, it is peculiarly damaging to concepts of total community education. In the case of community education we see children, parents, adults, and professional personnel all engaged in the process of learning together. Planning takes place on the part of entire groups.

143

Changes in plans occur from week to week and even day to day as results are measured and aim is taken on new goals. It is therefore a matter of highest importance that those engaged in the process of education be either free to move directly without special permission or at least be able to secure permission for change by a simple telephone call or written request, assuming that an answer will be forthcoming within a matter of hours.

TALL IS TO DIE, FLAT IS TO LIVE

There are, of course, other considerations that apply to all types of institutions. One is the matter of the origin of our existing administrative structure. Most of it has been borrowed from industry and the realm of military affairs. Vertical, tall, hierarchial organizations have assumed that planning and performance can be and should be separated. The tall organizational pattern has similarly assumed that teachers were relatively unprepared and that principals and supervisory personnel have the answers and could answer the questions. In a modern school organization, these assumptions are no longer valid. Not infrequently, teachers have more preparation than the principal or even the supervisory officer. Often the teachers are the best prepared persons in the school system. They may even be Master Teachers who on the basis of knowledge and preparation are the best persons in the school system to deal with the problem or provide an answer to a question. Yet in a highly vertical bureaucratic organization they must go through the same tiresome and frustrating process of getting permission from overhead officers. Our tendency has been to remove decision-making as far away from the child and the teacher as possible rather than to make the decision-making process an integral part of teaching and learning from day to day. In the field of medicine this mistake has not been made. It has been assumed that the practicing physician is the most competent person to decide. Hospital managers would not think of making decisions about drugs or surgical techniques and ordering physicians to use them or demanding that physicians seek permission in such matters.

The field of education has tended to copy the traditional industrial pattern rather than to take the cue from medical practice and from newer practices in business management which assign much more decision-making power to the individual practitioner. In any case, the old authoritarian pattern with layer upon layer of superstructure has become more and more oppressive and becomes especially oppressive to those school systems which set out to develop total community education programs which attempt to mobilize all the resources of the community and integrate the activities of both

144

professional and lay persons. The result is that, at the present moment, the traditional patterns of administration constitute a definite limit upon all innovative practices, including community education. Unless these practices can be changed, the process of achieving effective community education will be slowed to the point of ineffectiveness.

The tall, hierarchial, bureaucratic organizational patterns have repeatedly demonstrated that they are unable to cope with the educational problems endemic to their communities. This should be indictment enough to bring about drastic change in the organizational, administrative, decision-making structure of our large vertical school systems. However, the real indictment rests in the belief held by many teachers, parents and students, that not only is the present system incapable of solving the problems of our times, it is part of the problem.

VARIABILITY OF ENVIRONMENT

In the last decade, educators have become increasingly aware of the sharp differences that exist within a particular city or geographical area in the social and economic background of the children and the nature of the educational problems that must be faced. As a result of these wide differences between school districts and schools, general rules and regulations and requirements have become less and less applicable and indeed more and more destructive in their impact upon the whole educational process. Methodologies and curricular materials adaptable to a high income level community may be unusable in the ghetto. Teachers who do well with exceptional children may be very ineffective with children who present learning difficulties. In many areas, parents have lost much of their confidence in the school system. They are demanding a role in the control of the school and its policies and a chance to participate in the making of decisions. This demand takes the form of a request for decentralization and community control. These parents believe that policies in the school are basically antagonistic to the best interests of their children. They want to change the school and its practices. They have lost confidence in the school administration and the Board of Education and its capacity or willingness to adapt education to the needs of their particular children and to children in their geographical area. This demand on the part of parents has cut directly across the old pattern of administration and injected a new note into the old theory of educational administration. It is no wonder that the demands have been seen as controversial and that the process of working out a viable and effective way for parents to be involved in educational decisions is still to be done. However, in spite of the

145

controversy and the far reaching changes that are demanded by community involvement it is difficult to see how this movement can be turned back. In fact, it must somehow be facilitated and methods must be worked out which will preserve the integrity of the educative process, guarantee the welfare of the children's education and simultaneously enable teachers, parents and public to share in the decision-making process.

COLLECTIVE BARGAINING

The collective bargaining process has brought another counter force into the administrative structure. Decisions which were normally made by the Board of Education and executed by professional personnel are now becoming a part of the collective bargaining process. The absolute authority of the Boards of Education and the administrative personnel is being challenged. Decisions which used to be made by Superintendents and Principals are now made in the process of collective bargaining. Teachers are demanding the right to make these decisions a part of the collective bargaining process. In many instances, these demands cut across those made by the public and also across the more traditional practices of administrators so that the traditional school organization and the establishment is being attacked from several directions, by the teachers, by the parents and in some instances, particularly in higher education, by student activists. The demands for participation on the part of teachers, parents and students developed in no small measure as a result of the apparent failure of the traditional vertical organization to adapt itself with sufficient rapidity to new conditions. It is probably a safe assumption that no one connected with the educational establishment itself is really satisfied with the functioning of that establishment. More and more, teachers have become restive, parents have become dissatisfied, students have become insistent in their demand for a more relevant education and also for a chance to share in the shaping of that education.

A CREATIVE ADMINISTRATION

Even though the development of new concepts of administration may be a process fraught with controversy and many difficulties, such a development is paramount if true community education is to be developed. In fact, at the present moment, there are few factors in the building of community education more important than that of bringing about the necessary changes in administrative theory and practice. Not enough is known about the problem to be specific about the "how to" aspect. But there are some fundamental assumptions which are increasingly important.

First, the individual school and community must be seen as an educational unit with the freedom to adapt its program to the people of its area with their unique problems, backgrounds, economic level and cultural experience. In this way the principal of the individual school becomes a far more important decision-maker than he has been in past practice. It also means that more of the educational decision-making process must be flattened out and delegated to the principal and to the individual teachers and groups of teachers. It means more group planning with principals, teachers and parents, as well as children.

Second, it is very likely that the establishment of this principle in administration would reduce the need for the large central office staffs now characteristic of educational administration in our large cities. Moreover, the central office staffs would be increasingly seen as consultants, as specialists who function on call rather than as a level of administration between the principals and the superintendent and his staff.

Third, since the decision-making process will increasingly depend on professional competence and the capacity to listen to parents, teachers and children, it is clear that new demands will be made upon the preparation of principals and teachers. Increasingly in the process of decision-making, educators will be concerned with *what is right* rather than with the question *who is right*. For both teachers and principals skills in group process will become increasingly important, especially the capacity to listen.

Fourth, many of the activities carried on in the field of education can be done by lay people of various levels of competence and preparation as well as, and often better than by professional workers. It may hurt our professional pride, but it is becoming increasingly true that lay people are often more effective in various aspects of education than professional people themselves. One of the reasons for this situation is to be found in the increasing extent to which we recognize education as a human undertaking or as communication among human beings. People who live in a community can often communicate better with other people who live in that community than teachers and administrators who have had a very different experience and who for this reason find communication rather difficult.

Fifth, the touchstone is *freedom* . . . freedom to think, to create, to give, to receive, to experience. What does anyone in the central office know about the new turn of events in the Lincoln School, about the car salesman who has become a youth leader, the mother who has developed a real passion for helping non-readers or about the new spirit of higher expectation in the Jones family?

Vertical organizations, directives from the downtown office, adopted textbooks, grades, marking systems . . . all are in the way . . . obstructions to the development of a learning community.

Sixth, in community education the need is for a flat organization in which flexibility, adaptation, search for new ideas are the watchwords. We need an organization in which we can take in a new member today, listen to him and let him help us probe a problem. The Staff in Community Education is not sharply defined, it changes from day to day. It is more like an artists colony than like a factory. It is a community in which it is exciting to work. "I wake up in the morning with a new idea. I can't wait until I can try it out on my colleagues, because I know they will be receptive. My expectation is they will expand it, give it new dimensions or perhaps be stimulated to propose an even more exciting idea."

Seventh, in community education we need group leadership, for essentially we are groups solving problems together. In conventional administration, ideas are expected to come from the leader. We often speak of Mr. Murphy's program. "Are you for it or against it?" "It is obviously not my program or your program." In the new flat group-oriented organization individuals are not dependent on the one great leader. The leader is not required or expected to have all the ideas, a solution for every problem. His *know how* consists of *knowing how* to create "the climate" in which all members of the group are encouraged to be creative. When people are free to dream, when they can make their dreams visible without fear, there will be no dearth of ideas.

The basic fact that all members of an organization confront is *change*. With change comes the need for new processes, new methodologies, new attitudes. Open groups do not fear change, they are not threatened, they find change exciting, a stimulus to creative thought and action.

Bennis gives the following conditions for a collaborative group climate:

Flexible and adaptive structure, utilization of individual talents, clear and agreed upon goals, standards of openness, trust and cooperation, interdependence, high intrinsic rewards and transactional controls, which means a lot of individual autonomy and a lot of participation in making key decisions. [1]

Executive leadership must take some responsibility in creating a climate that provides the security to identify with the adaptive process without fear of losing status. [2]

It is not easy for superintendents and principals who have grown up in the old vertical organization to adapt themselves to the type of leadership community education demands. Distribution of decision-making often threatens such leaders. They have to learn how to share, share power and share credit for accomplishment. They have to acquire the humility to listen, to function as a member of a group, to admit they are at times wrong, to grant the superiority of others, to be ready to discard their own proposals for those of others if these are found more desirable.

One of the reasons it is so hard for administrators to adopt group decision-making grows out of our traditional practice of personalizing both administrative failure and success. If a principal loses his position, we assume it is his personal failure. If a superintendent is fired, we hold post-mortems on his failure . . . detailing his personal shortcomings. In all this, we overlook the fact that the organization of which he was a part was at fault. Instead of examining the system, we search for a new superintendent only to fire him a few years later. This process goes on destroying one individual after the other while we learn nothing about the unsound theory on which these executives have tried to function and the flaws in the organization which handicap every executive.

In total community education, the centralized, personalized executive type of organization is especially inappropriate, ineffective and dysfunctional. It does not produce the climate needed for human growth. Bennis describes the newer group approach to leadership as "an active method for producing conditions where people and ideas and resources can be seeded, cultivated and integrated to optimum effectiveness and growth." [3]

---

[1] Bennis, Warren G. "Post Bureaucratic Leadership," *Transaction*, July-August 1969, p. 47.
[2] *Ibid.*, pp. 48-49
[3] *Ibid.*, p. 51

Administrators need to be counseled that sharing of decision-making gives greater strength to the organization and fosters a more comfortable relationship. There is greater satisfaction, too, since the success of others and the success of the enterprise is promoted. The feeling of loneliness that is experienced by most traditional administrators would disappear since the creative talents of all could be released in the interest of the total school development.

THE ROLE OF THE COMMUNITY SCHOOL IN DECENTRALIZATION

There can be no question that the current demand for community control has been intensified by the bureaucratic nature of educational administration especially in our large cities. It is thus a reaction to the oppressive effect of excessive centralization. The problem is: How can people be involved in the educative process in such a way that we can get their judgment, their contribution without turning the control of the educational program over to narrow parochial and self-serving groups on a narrow community basis? It is at this point that community education appears to supply a partial answer.

Over the last quarter century, there have been conditions with respect to the control of education that have been disappointing. Parents have not been regular participants in the school program. They have had too little contact with teachers and principals. They have not been consulted individually, nor in groups. Students and citizens have not been involved in planning. This lack of participation has resulted in poor support for education in general. Greater participation upon the part of all within the community will result in better control and the marshaling of the community's assets for the educational effort.

In our democratic society we think often of the process of voting as a means of making decisions. While this works well in the choice of elected officials, it does not lend itself to the discovery of the best processes in the field of education. A method of teaching reading is not necessarily best because the people of a community vote for it, anymore than a drug in the treatment of a disease is effective because a poll taken on its merits suggests that two-thirds of the people believe it is the best remedy. In areas such as education and medicine, the question is not the popularity of a method or process but the scientific evidence concerning its merits. In fact, in such areas it is highly desirable not to vote on too many matters but to provide full and frequent discussion with the development of a consensus growing out of the daily experience of the persons involved. It is just such daily and broad experience that community schools make possible. Too often at present school authorities bring decisions regarding steps to be taken from the outside, resulting in materials and methods that do not fit the needs of the children nor the realities of the community. There is little provision for listening to parents with regard to their views in these matters. Parents have a feeling that teachers and principals are remote and lacking in understanding. There are few channels for "give and take" between lay and professional people. The professional workers themselves are too much controlled by directives from central offices and by professional materials which have little applicability to a given situation.

True community education studies its own community. It seeks to meet the wants and needs of the people who live in this community. It sets out to understand them and to adapt its programs to their current educational status. In teaching, there is an effort to begin with the children where they are, to begin with the people of the community in terms of their present understanding of educational problems. There is every faith that in this way, both the children and their parents will grow in educational understanding and that the nature of the program will change from time to time as growth is experienced by young and more mature people.

This kind of administration rests on faith in the people of the community and faith in the teachers, the children and their parents. It rests on the assumption that people can be trusted to develop their own criteria of truth and value if they are given an opportunity to view the problem and to make choices. Thousands of teachers and principals throughout America know that this is true. It is really surprising that in view of the many success stories we have in this area, they have made so little impact on general educational administrative practice and have to such a small degree found their way into administrative theory and practice.

It does not take much imagination to see that the horizontal organizational pattern visualized in this volume requires a radical change in the attitude of administrative personnel and also in the attitudes of teachers. It will not be so easy for teachers to dodge an issue by merely saying to the principal: What do you want me to do? It will not be so simple for the principal to decide an issue on the basis of administrative fiat. If the teacher and the principal are both involved with the parents and the children in an actual learning situation they will be forced to consider the realities of that situation and to make their decisions accordingly.

One of our current difficulties in the field of educational administration is that we have overstressed the managerial, clerical and organizational aspects of the educational leader's task. The result is that many of our administrators have lost any real sense of intellectual or human leadership. Instead, they merely push papers, send memos to each other, answer telephones and carry keys from one room to another. Their role has become clerical, custodial and authoritarian. Their foot is on the brake rather than on the accelerator. The key to change lies in the word "freedom": freedom for principals, teachers, parents and for children. *True* community education mobilizes resources of the community and sets them free.

PERSONALITY AND BEHAVIORAL PATTERNS

While the organizational patterns characteristic of most school systems in America are in conflict with the development of the type of educational programs needed, the organizational patterns themselves and the administrative theories upon which they are based have led to the growth of certain qualities of personality and types of behavior that militate against total community education and its effective leadership. Experience in community schools, observation of the work of principals, community school directors, teachers and citizens provide guidelines for the personality qualities and patterns of behavior which liberate human beings. The authors have the temerity to state these in the form of:

TEN SUGGESTIONS FOR ADMINISTRATORS

1. Respect all the people with whom you work, children, parents, teachers and people generally.

2. Believe in people, trust them and care about them.

3. Keep people well-informed, maintaining an open administration and an open door to all, being especially considerate and thoughtful to the disadvantaged and to those with little power.

4. Do not form or work with cliques. Plan and carry out your work so as to bring people together and avoid actions and attitudes which drive them apart.

5. Behave in such a way that people will feel free to come to you for help.

6. Welcome all criticism and suggestions. Be sure to receive all who bring suggestions and criticisms in such a way that they will never regret having come to you.

7. Assume that all want to do better, that they wish to improve themselves and their work and are really trying to help you.

8. Be humble. Humility is the strongest armor one can have against critical opposition. "A soft answer turneth away wrath."

9. Be optimistic, emphasizing the positive aspects of people and situations. Avoid being a prophet of gloom. Do not bring your personal problems to work. The people with whom you work have a right to expect a dynamic, vigorous, and enlightened leadership.

10. Be generous in giving credit to others for success, seeking to bring visibility to your colleagues and being wary of seeking the limelight for yourself.

The traditional impression which remains in the mind of many is a picture of the administrator as one who is cold, distant, withdrawn, and reluctant to praise people for good work. Too often administrators tend to close their doors. They are reluctant to divulge information about the enterprise as a whole and slow to delegate responsibility and include people in decision-making. All of these tendencies, characteristics and behavior patterns thwart leadership in community education, because in total community education everybody is on the team. We desire whole-hearted cooperation and a feeling of belonging which is difficult to acquire unless the personality, characteristics and behavior patterns of administrators are such as to produce them.

NEED FOR ENTHUSIASTIC LEADERSHIP

It is a paradox that in America where advertising and public relations have been carried to a high level of development that so little has rubbed off on the educational leadership. American administrative leadership in the field of education is notedly hesitant, timid and lacking in conviction and enthusiasm. Generally speaking, we do not act as if we were completely sold on the enterprise in which we are engaged. Educators complain about personal and professional obstacles far too much. The prevailing estimate of human potential is far too low. Too often a heavy academic involvement seems to have made us dull and pedantic, and caused us to lose our capacity to communicate with people about education in language and approaches that reach the minds and hearts of people. In part, this is due to the fact that as school people we have lived too much within the schoolhouse, too much confined to people like ourselves and out of daily communication with different groups of people with varying insights into the nature of problems and solutions.

The size of our educational institutions has something to do with this development. School systems and universities are so large that they have become a world unto themselves. It becomes difficult for educational personnel to escape the very mass of the enterprise in which they are engaged in order to make contact with people in other areas. Such contact is vital in any case but especially important in the totality of community education. Educators need to learn how to relate to many different types of people. More than this, we need to learn how to utilize community personnel in establishing the relationships which we as administrators find difficult to achieve.

One might summarize this by pointing out that the educational enterprise is the way it is because we have not done what we ought to be doing. We have lived in too circumscribed an environment, reached too few people, made contacts with too narrow a spectrum of community groups. Were we to enlarge the scope of our activities, widen the range of the groups of people with whom we maintain relationships, the effect of all this would change our behavior and our attitude. Thus, community education is not only a means of educating children and parents but is also a means of educating school personnel, teachers, principals and superintendents. Our problem is to get educators at all levels to take the first steps which will bring about their involvement in the community. Once this involvement takes place, changed attitudes will be forthcoming.

CHAPTER XI

MOBILIZING AND INVOLVING COMMUNITY RESOURCES

Mobilizing and Involving Community Resources

INTRODUCTION

If the decade of the sixties is to be distinguished by any development in the field of education, it is surely that of a greater realization of the richness of the educational resources of the community. During this decade educators and lay people alike have become aware of the fact that many activities and processes in education can be performed as well by relatively untrained parents and citizens as by specialists. Many schools make use of extensive teacher aides. In addition, evening and adult programs utilize persons in the community who, while they may not have teacher's certificates and be professionally qualified in the usual sense, have skills and capacities that help them to be active and creative participants in the total program. The discovery of the power of lay participants in education may well be the most important educational discovery of many decades.

In community education the potential of lay participants opens a new vista of achievement. This is not only because total community education makes heavy demands on personnel for leadership and teaching, but what is more important is that we have discovered that teaching is perhaps the best way to learn. Consequently an entirely new constellation of resources and educational tasks has arisen. It works something like this: Everyone in the community needs further education. This applies fully as much to teachers and university professors as it does to citizens generally. At the same time this need for further education could not possibly be met were we dependent on professional personnel alone. But the moment we discover that lay people in the community have a contribution to make a new vista of resources has been opened to us. When it is further discovered that all who participate in a teaching or leadership capacity are in the process of undergoing education themselves, we finally discover that the line between those who teach and those who are being taught virtually disappears.

For many decades school people have tried to develop interest on the part of the public in our schools. The Parent-Teacher Associations, school programs and many other devices have been efforts to interest the public. None of these efforts has been entirely successful. The reason is that in virtually all of these efforts the public has sensed that it was on the receiving end. Citizens were being educated, informed and sometimes brain-washed by professional people. Citizens did not feel that they were contributors to education but rather that they were being asked to assume financial responsibility and give carte blanche backing to professional people. In all of this, they sensed a feeling of inferiority in comparison with the professional teacher.

If you go to a citizen and suggest that he ought to take a course, the implication is that he needs further education. This may be something of a blow to his ego and may account for the difficulty in persuading many people to take part in adult education. But if the same person is asked to come to the school and help with a program for children or youth, you are doing something to build his ego and in all probability he will feel complimented that he has been asked. Experiences in recent years in community schools bear out this point in striking ways. Throughout the country in our community school experience hundreds of parents and citizens have become involved and in the process have built their own interests in further education as well as developed a better self image and a better understanding of education generally.

Past efforts to explain education to citizens by speeches, bulletins, articles in the press and the like have not been notably successful. This may well be due to the fact that education is such a subtle undertaking, involves so many nuances and depends so heavily upon actual experience that the only way in which one can really acquire true educational understanding is to be a participant in the process.

Growing dissatisfaction on the part of parents and citizens with the achievement of children in schools particularly in disadvantaged areas has led to renewed demands for community involvement in the making of educational decisions. Thus, the movement in community education is in a strategic position to deal with the problem from at least two different points of view. In the first place total community education can involve the parents and citizens in such a way that they will have a true feeling that they are participants in the total process and can assist in the making of decisions in relation to it. In addition, through this process the citizens will play a better role since they will acquire a better understanding of education and its problems.

THE COMMUNITY AS AN EDUCATIONAL INSTRUMENTALITY

In discussing the role of the community in education we run afoul of a vicious circularity. It is the community that educates, yet we are also aware of the erosion of the community as an educational agent. Another way to say it is that we need a good community to have good education but at the very time when this need is greatest we are rapidly losing a sense of community. It may help at this point to inquire into the meaning of community and in turn analyze in greater detail the process of erosion. The aim is to understand the community in order that we can mount an educational program which simultaneously seeks to build community and utilize the community that is in process of its improvement as an educational agency. We believe programs can be built which make the community's participation in education an educational means for building a better community.

There are numbers of definitions of the word community. For our purposes the definition used by Newman and Oliver seems helpful.

A community is a group:

1. in which membership is valued as an end in itself, not merely as a means to other ends;

2. that concerns itself with many and significant aspects of the lives of members;

3. that allows competing factions;

4. whose members share commitment to common purpose and to procedures for handling conflict within the group;

5. whose members share responsibility for the actions of the group;
6. whose members have enduring and extensive personal contact with each other. [1]

If one views the modern city with the above definition in mind he will immediately sense that urban areas have lost much of their reality as a community. In the modern city, high specialization separates the individual from his neighbor and relates him, if at all, to the membership of his specialty. It is more difficult for him to understand his neighbors if they belong to another specialty. One can see it plainly in the university. Members of faculties of different departments find it harder and harder to communicate, taking an increasingly narrow view of the various problems. Because of the high educational level and above average training in communication one might expect this to be a smaller problem in academic circles, but day to day movement in specialized areas seems to deny this.

The black power movement is an excellent example of the way in which fragmentation, rapid social change, excessive emphasis on material values, and depersonalization have all combined to give the individual a feeling of being powerless to change the situation in which he finds himself. It can thus be said that the black power movement is more a reaction to the fact of being without power than it is a reach for power over others, a really defensive rather than an offensive concept.

It would, however, be a mistake to see the powerless feeling as being associated only with poor people or black people. It affects people at all economic levels. How often one hears prominent people in the community speak of the violence in our cities, only to follow with the remark, "Well, there is nothing we can do," or, "You can't fight city hall." Suburbs, too, have become areas in which a community feeling has been eroded.

A look at a high economic level suburb may be helpful. It is populated mainly by families who are upward mobile, who are seeking to escape the evils of the central city, or seeking the higher prestige that comes from living in Rolling Hills as compared to Akron. They have already made many of their friendships, hence do not try very hard to learn to know the people in the new neighborhood. Only in a crisis, such as a massive zoning change, will they get together and find common cause. The children, the teenagers though,

---

[1] Fred M. Newman and Donald W. Oliver, "Education and Community", *Harvard Educational Review*, Vol. 37, Winter 1967. pp. 61-106.

will perforce make new friends. Many a suburban parent has learned to know his neighbors through the involvement of his son or daughter in a tragedy or an unfortunate incident.

Most often the suburban resident is still making his living in the central city. In many cases, he has been an important contributor to the life of the city. Now his interests are shifted to his haven of refuge in the bedroom community. The city he has left behind (as a place to live) has been weakened, both in material and human resources. In turn, the suburb is acquiring citizens who want to create a little circle of their own, who fear that poor people and especially black people will move into the suburb. Their attitude becomes more and more exclusive. They become more and more involved in a kind of privatism. Often their own suburban communities are lacking in many types of joint effort for community betterment but anyone who raises his voice to outline community needs often is seen as a trouble maker. Having gone to considerable effort to escape the central city and having seen his move to the suburb as an upward move, the typical suburbanite does not like to hear that the area to which he has moved is lacking in desirability.

No effort is being made here to find fault with suburban living or suburban residents. The posit here is to indicate that virtually all areas in our society are affected by the loss of community which has accompanied technological development. In rural areas, farms are larger so that neighbors are farther away. Mobility is increasing rapidly here too.

"Decentralists" have inveighed against the city for decades. Their arguments are persuasive but about the only public response has been an increasing trend toward urbanization. The great metropolitan areas are growing rapidly and the central cities are either decreasing in population or barely holding their own. Since there is little likelihood that there will be any significant change in the trends, there seems little to be gained by just deploring concentration of population. A more productive course is to build educational and other community agencies that will function so as to reduce the "missing sense of community" and supply it through the medium of total community education.

A NEW BALL GAME

The moment we set out to educate the entire community we are in a new ball game. We no longer can be separated into two groups, teachers and students, for we are all teachers and students. Some will teach as a life work, others will teach merely to learn (teaching being the best way to learn), or at least learn in the process of teaching. The administrative problems now become more complex, with the result that the old separation of planning and performance concepts break down. Control by status personnel now must be exercised with the greatest care lest it limit the freedom of all to learn. Where in the past we have too often asked *who* is right, we must now ask *what* is right. We need to learn how to listen and how to understand.

Increasingly we see that we have something to learn from the ecologists. For example, Richard E. Farson suggests that instead of trying so hard to change people we should try changing the total environment in such ways that the environment stimulates behavioral changes. He further suggests that:

> *Instead of looking to a professional elite for the solution to any social problem, look to the greatest resource available . . . the very population that has the problem. Many of us tend to have a low opinion of people, those wretched masses who don't understand, don't know what they need or want, who continually make mistakes and foul up their lives, requiring those of us who are professionally trained to come in and correct the situation. But that is not the way it really works. The fact is that some drug addicts are much better able to cure addiction in each other than are psychiatrists; some convicts can run better rehabilitation programs for convicts than do correctional officers; many students tend to learn more from each other than from many professors; some patients in mental hospitals are better for each other than is the staff. Thousands of self-help organizations are doing a good job, perhaps a better job at problem-solving than is the profession that is identified with that problem. People who have the problems often have a better understanding of their situation and what must be done to change it. What professionals have to do is learn to cooperate with that resource to design the conditions which evoke that intelligence.* [2]

> *In this way, society can be truly self-determining and self-renewing. The special beauty of this formulation is that it fits the democratic goal of enabling the people to make a society for themselves. Mankind can rely on people as a resource for much more than is possible to imagine. It is really quite difficult to find the ceiling of what people can do for themselves and each other, given the opportunity.* [3]

[2] Richard E. Farson, "How Could Anything That Feels So Bad Be So Good", *The Saturday Review*, Sept. 6, 1969, p. 20.

[3] *Ibid.*

Farson thus sets forth a philosophical premise for a successful program of total community education. Such a program must rest on faith in people and their capacity to learn. Administration in such a program must design the conditions which increase intelligence and proceed by cooperating with all the community resources. Present preparation for administrators helps them deal with the people they control, but their success in total community education depends more on their ability to deal effectively with the people they do not control than those they do control. The tools of the past administration are legalism, rules, regulations and line and staff authority. This same administration is too often short on inspiration, on freedom of action and too often frowns on innovation. It is short on faith in people.

Community involvement cannot be merely attached to our present obsolete administrative structure. To do this can lead to dysfunctional conditions for education with frustration of all concerned. We need a new theory and practice of administration designed for total community education, an education in which all the people of the community are involved. Such education mandates community *involvement* in educational programs. However, complete community *control* of education could mean a narrow provincial, even racist education for some communities. Such a development could surely be a threat to true democratic education.

In some areas further centralization is in process and to be desired. We need, for example, to give the federal government a larger share in defining equality of educational opportunity and in the support of education necessary to give economic substance to the goals of equal opportunity we set. The same is true of the states and their role.

The task of designing a concept of educational administration attuned to the needs of education in our time should not be viewed as a mere technical exercise. The project must be undertaken with a full realization of how far our society has already gone toward what John Gardner [4] calls the beehive model, how restrictive many of our gigantic institutions of industry, government and education have become, and how isolated and helpless large numbers of our people have become. The organization we design and develop in practice must so energize the profession and the people of the nation, that we will build an education that will give our people greater commitment to our historic values. Only in this way can we bring the individual human-being greater justice, deeper sense of brotherhood, equality of opportunity, sense of his own, as well as of other's dignity and worth and a larger feeling of social responsibility. Seen in the light of such an educational goal for our nation, community involvement, rather than being viewed as a threat should be seen as a great challenge. In fact, if through community involvement we can mobilize the vast resources for education now found in every community, we can open a new era in educational achievement and new levels of democratic living for our society.

THE COMMUNITY EDUCATION CONCEPT

The great aim of education is not knowledge but action.

Herbert Spencer

Up to this point we have discussed the needs of communities, the lack of a sense of community, a condition that characterizes so much of modern America. To a large measure one question still haunts the authors: Has the community education idea come alive in the minds of the reader? For many the answer, we are sure, is a resounding "no"! The idea is sound to many but how does one implement a true community education philosophy?

Past experience in writing and speaking about community education reveals that many individuals do not get the true impact, a real feeling for community education until they are surrounded by a program in action. Visitors to community education programs in Flint, Michigan; Miami, Florida; Phoenix, Arizona; Atlanta, Georgia; Toledo, Ohio; New Haven, Connecticut; to mention only a few, come away dazed by the eloquent simplicity and magnificent accomplishments of these programs. Visitors to true community education programs come away awed by what they have seen. Yet they are often bewildered by the enormity and complexity of the programs in operation. It is not unusual for visitors to community education programs to find thousands of people in a given school on a given evening. How are such programs started? How are they organized? How are they financed? These are all "nuts and bolts" that need answering. Readers in search of a set of prescriptions that are applicable to all communities will be disappointed in this publication. Prescriptions for a successful program, a set itinerary, a grab bag of tricks are not in the offering. To attempt to prescribe one program for

164

all communities would destroy the vitality and the relevance of a program that is geared to serving a community's wants and needs. The process of local and personal involvement is fundamental to community education. Community education is a process, not an end in itself.

Community education is much easier to describe than it is to define. A community education program, to begin with, is not a program that begins when the regular school day ends. To think of community education as a separate program superimposed upon existing school destroys the concept at its inception. To think in terms of community education as a simple extension of an obsolete educational system that has serious problems and is in danger of falling as a result of its own dead weight is also a misconception. Extending the existing educational program is not the answer to a successful community education program until there are dramatic changes in the existing structure of our present day schools. One should not visualize a community school program as frosting placed on the existing educational cake. Community education is "the cake" . . a new cake. Community education envisions a new educational cake, Education II, with a new recipe, new ingredients and totally new dimensions. Further, it is important to note that community education programs are not always centered in the schoolhouse. At one time a book may have been sufficient to make school exciting. In these times, "bookish" education becomes dull in the context of the exciting communities in which the pupils live. The action is outside the four walls of the school building. The community . . . that's where the action is! . . . To confine children and adults to the four walls of the school building is to artificially stifle achievement, creativity and awareness.

There are, of course, exceptions but they may tend to further illustrate the obsolescence of the schoolhouse brand of education rather than defend it. In one community the authors had the pleasure of viewing an exciting open space, open school concept for first graders. The setting was a large room that once contained the 1920 version of bolted down seats which had been duly removed and converted into a community in microcosm for first graders. For the approximately one hundred and fifty first graders the result was an exciting world. The classroom contained a village store, a library, a Montessori inspired arithmetic laboratory and a host of small groups in interaction. But as exciting as this is for first and even for second graders these children will soon outgrow this miniature world and will want broader and deeper experiences that cannot be provided in a classroom or even on an extensive educational campus.

Another misconception regarding community education is to view it as another layer of the existing educational cake. This notion has often led communities to accept a series of cookbook courses, i.e. ceramics, adult basic reading programs and a few added recreational programs. In short, an extended school day concept is used as a substitute for true community education. Community education is a new concept with new dimensions. It's power lies in the changes it demands of the fundamental and traditional assumptions of what constitutes an education. Possibly the best way to get a true feeling for community education is to analyze the anatomy and spirit of a school that centers around a new position in education, that of community school director. Visitors to community schools are often greeted at the front door by a young professional educator, often called the Community School Director. Possibly his title is Community Agent or Assistant to the Principal for Community Education. His title is not important. His function is what makes the difference for the emerging profession that he represents. The Community School Director is responsible directly to the school Principal. He generally reports to school in the early afternoon and becomes actively involved with programs for students, faculty and members of the community. Realizing that the success of a community education program hinges on his leadership in bringing students, faculty and community into a meaningful juxtaposition, the director spends his early afternoon hours acting as a catalytic agent. He's a good listener, he listens to merchants in the community, visits with the faculty and makes house calls. He serves as the cybernetic agent for his school. He provides feedback, listens, communicates and makes plans for actions that are relevant to the needs and wants expressed by the different elements of the community. He is not an empire builder, he's a coordinator, a facilitator of existing functions and agencies. To fulfill the role, the community school director listens and learns . . what are the needs of the people in this community? . . what agencies in this community are dedicated toward providing these services? . . what about the boy that needs eye glasses and can't afford them? How can we involve the Lions Club that is dedicated to providing corrective lenses for the unfortunate? He is at the grass root level and makes it his job to know about needs and services and to bring the two together. Some have compared this aspect of the community directors role to the "ombudsman" found in Scandinavian countries. One of the ironies of our time is the high level of humanitarian effort on the part of both public and private sectors of our society and the lack of communication with individuals and families that have the most need for these services. The community director is then a catalyst for all education, and education is interpreted in its broadest sense to include social, recreational, cultural, and educational activities for all ages. The director is keenly aware of the educational program that exists during the regular school hours. He is also aware of the needs and wants of the community. He is a student of social service. He accepts the responsibility for bringing together people who have never interacted under a traditional educational structure. He is assisting the administration and faculty and informing the community of the goals and aspirations of the school program. The information and feedback is now a two-way street. The community school director informs, shares information, and educates the administration and faculty regarding the issues, problems and most important resources that are available in the community. In this volume we have called for Education II, a new education that will require a new concept of the role of teachers and a new concept of the role of the community. The community school director must exemplify the artistry that is demanded of new educators in Education II. He must be a reader, a listener and a learner. He leads through example. As an educator of tomorrow, he must possess a scholarly and down-to-earth knowledge of learning theory as it relates to school and community. Knowledge of a particular subject matter is not enough. As a professional educator he must come to grips with the key issues in education which revolve around: How a child learns; What are the significant forces which foster the learning process? What evidence can he bring to bear on the problems of learning when it is paralleled into its three principal ingredients: motivation, transfer and the self concept.

There is a critical need today for a redefinition of the processes of learning. The *proficient* school director can intelligently discuss the theories of learning. He is constantly analyzing the basic assumptions concerning the nature of man. He is a student of psychology, sociology and human behavior. The Community Director is a teacher and a teacher is a learner:

> The teacher studies philosophy.
> The teacher studies each pupil.
> The teacher studies learning.
> The teacher studies instruction.
> The teacher studies himself.
> The teacher studies his world.
> The teacher studies our heritage of freedom.
> The teacher studies his subject.

ANATOMY OF A COMMUNITY SCHOOL

The community school is the focal point of a community education program. It is hazardous to attempt to reduce a community school program to a set of components. Components can be misinterpreted as prescriptions for instant success, leaving the true affective meaning waiting in the wings. However, it is equally dangerous to remain too vague. With this note of caution, what then are the ingredients or components that comprise the modern community school? Experience would indicate that a minimum of twelve ingredients, components or concerns are present in an effective community school program.

Component I:

Maximized Use of Existing Human and Physical Resources

Community education and its vehicle for action, the community school, set forth a new set of assumptions regarding the setting, purpose, task and role of the school. To begin with, it searches for an education that is relevant to the needs of all clients in the community served. The community school has a broader definition of client than the traditional school. In Education II, the community school, all members of the community are clients.

Education I, has limited its perception of clients, curricula offerings and school services to a narrow context. For example, school plants, sites and faculty and community resources have been limited to:

— School aged children and young adults
— A five day school week
— A 39 to 40 week school year
— A six to seven hour school day
— Programs and services for school aged children with little or no concern for the educational, recreational, cultural or social wants and needs of the total community.

The first component of the new education, is the broadening of school programs and services, so that they encompass the entire community. This new dimension:

— Includes all age groups
— Opens schools on weekends
— Opens school year-round
— Opens schools from early morning until late evening, and in some communities leaves them open around the clock.

The educational umbrella and all its integral parts is enlarged and extended to embrace the entire community. The community, in a sense, becomes a giant classroom and all members of the community are invited to participate as teachers and learners. Once the philosophy that underpins community education is accepted, education takes on some new and exciting dimensions.

Component II:

Establishment of Cooperative Procedures with Governmental Service Agencies

There are literally hundreds of tax-supported governmental agencies, federal, state and local dedicated to the accepted educational objectives of the schools. Programs financed by various agencies with tax dollars have been "shot-gunned" throughout communities. Separate bureaucracies have been established. Efforts of humanitarian services and client centered agencies often overlap, are duplicated and are fragmented.

Community school plants, sites, playground and facilities serve as the focal point for community services. The modern community school shares its resources with other client-centered agencies and actively seeks the cooperation of all other government agencies dedicated toward improving educational, economic, cultural, recreational and social life in the community.

The community school staff works in close cooperation with other government agencies:

Some Illustrations:

— State and Local Libraries
— Division of Adult Education
— Division of Vocational Education (Vocational Education Act 1963)
— State employment security commission (Manpower Development & Training Act 1961) (MOTA)
— City, County, State Parks and Recreation Departments
— Commission on Aging
— Director of NDEA (National Defense Education Act)
— Director of ESEA (Elementary & Secondary Education Act)
— Veterans Administration
— Local & State Office of Economic Opportunity (Economic Opportunity Act 1964)
— Local & State Departments of Family Services
— Local & State Departments of Health
— Job Corps
— Teacher Corps

169

- Head Start Programs
- Neighborhood Youth Corps
- Law Enforcement Agencies
- Public Safety Agencies
- Housing and Urban Development
- Volunteers In-Service to America (VISTA)
- Adult Basic Education Programs
- Programs for the Foreign Born
- State Extension Services
- Department of Agriculture

The above agencies and many others are dedicated to the same goals and to services to people. There is a need to coordinate the efforts and utilize the resources of such agencies at the local, grass root level. The schools for too long have tried to go it alone. The schools are not alone in their short-sightedness. Most of these agencies have also elected to go it alone. Thus, duplicating facilities, staff and overhead expenses. The public interest, in many cases, seems to have been neglected. Well established agencies have been reluctant to share their spheres of influence or power. The loser in this fragmented approach to community problems has been those in need of the services and the taxpayer.

The suggestion here is not that the school develop a super-hierarchy embracing all the above services. This would be disastrous and negate the plea for a flat, operation-centered organizational pattern, that places the decision-making as close to the operational level as possible.

Rather it is a suggestion that the community school become a human resource center through which all the above agencies might funnel their resources to the grass root or operational level.

Component III:

Establishment of Cooperative Procedures with Volunteer and Civic Service Organizations

Foreign visitors to our shores are amazed at the number and scope of civic and humanitarian minded organizations, clubs and agencies that exist in every community in these United States. The traditional school has to a large extent ignored the human and physical and moral support that is available. The modern community schools call on these agencies for support and cooperate with them in their educational, cultural and recreational efforts.

Some Illustrations:

— Red Cross
— YMCA
— YWCA
— Jaycee
— Service Clubs
— Civic Clubs
— Big Brothers of America
— National Safety Council
— Boy and Girl Scouts
— Veteran Groups
— Women's Clubs

The civic and service organizations of every community need the resources of the schools and the schools need the resources of the community. By bringing the various service, civic organizations and the schools into closer juxtaposition we find the Community School Concept giving a dynamism to all conce·ned.

Component IV

The Development of Cooperative Procedures with Business and Industry

The community school makes a concerted effort to mobilize, coordinate and utilize the resources of business and industry. In many areas, most of our readers know of specific instances where business and industry have attempted to cooperate, to innovate, and to contribute to the local educational effort and have been rebuffed. Business and industry have deep concerns and interests in good education. However, they are seldom asked by local schools for intellectual or human input. We have restricted our requests for support from business and industry to requests for additional tax dollars. This is understandable since this is the approach we have used with citizens in general. The requests for additional tax dollars can be interpreted as an appeal for additional support so that the schools might continue to go it alone! The closed educational system then continues to pour money into what many members of the community consider to be meaningless activities. As an illustration, schools continue to purchase more and more woodworking machinery for woodshops often under the pretense that they are offering meaningful vocational experiences for their class. Wood working experiences may be interpreted in todays age as a meaningful avocation or hobby. However, it is difficult to justify the inordinate emphasis placed in this area in a society that has moved to synthetics, plastics, electronics and sophisticated metals.

One reason we have not developed more cooperative procedures with this industry is simply because the schools cannot accept or utilize the expertise available in these institutions because the personnel is not *certified*. Business and industry, in turn, is often reluctant to accept the certified personnel the school has to offer. The school's "certified" personnel may not be abreast of modern developments or the goals and objectives of business and industry. The problem then becomes circular. Education II proposes a reappraisal of school certification policies. Education must find ways to use the talents of business and industry in the school and at the same time through a concentrated effort of staff development prepare educators to work in close cooperation with the practitioners in the business and industrial world of work.

Acceptance of new approaches to education, the acceptance of new dimensions of cooperation has important implications with respect to educational personnel, educational facilities and student assignments. If the entire community is viewed as a classroom, new vistas present themselves in terms of additional classrooms and additional teaching personnel. Classes are held in industrial plants and in business establishments. Business and industry cooperate by sending instructors to the local schools. Student assignments take on new meanings. Busses crisscross the community. Students are bussed to educational sites for educational programs and they are not always in the schoolhouse. Bussing is done to promote the primary goal of education. It is not an exercise to create a racial mixture which many feel tends to exaggerate racial differences. It becomes a process designed to work for equality of opportunity regardless of race, religion, or national origin.

Component V:

The Establishment of Cooperative Procedures with Other Educational Institutions

The modern community school is constantly in search of new methods to utilize and cooperate with the services offered by other educational institutions both private and public within the community. The community school becomes a laboratory for university research. Faculties of the local schools and universities cooperatively develop procedures for staff development. University students are presented with new avenues to become involved in local programs and to contribute to their educational goals. Two excellent examples of the above are the cooperative procedures developed between community schools and the college work-study programs and the VISTA programs that exist in many communities.

The community school becomes a satellite for other educational institutions in the community. University continuing education classes and community college classes are offered in the community schools. The community school publicizes the vocational training programs available in the community. If needed, the community school acts as an agent to arrange for and serve as a convenient focal point for car pools or bus transportation to other educational facilities. Educational and vocational guidance is offered in and through the community school program. In essence, the community school concept tries to bridge the gap that exists between elementary and secondary education and the technical and liberal arts programs of higher educational institutions. The need for this type of service is apparent in all communities. However, it is exaggerated and intensified in communities that serve the lower social economic segments of each community.

Component VI:

The Establishment of Procedures for Self-generating Activities

The community school establishes policies and provisions through which each community can help itself. Each school community has unique and particular wants and needs. Accompanying these indigenous wants and needs, each school community has unique resources and talents. The community school establishes procedures that allow programs to begin upon individual and group requests. Interested individuals and groups are not confined to a quarter or semester system. Class programs, activities and special events can begin when people begin to feel the need. In the community school, programs are not dependent upon federal, state or local allocations. Procedures are established through a *community education revolving account* which allows and encourages unique programs supported by local contributions, fees, tuitions or volunteer services.

For example, procedures are established whereby a group of interested citizens may request activities, or classes involving Bridge, Dancing, Fishing, Dog Obedience, Fur Restoration, Literary Societies, Folk Culture, and

173

the like. The school then provides these opportunities on a revolving non-profit community self-supporting basis. It is further assumed under this premise that the community has paid for the use of the school through their tax support. Fees and tuitions are levied only on those particular aspects of the program that serve individual interests. To charge rent, to add additional fees for the use of school equipment or to prorate the cost of lighting, air conditioning and janitorial services for community use of the school is the antithesis of community education.

Component VII:

The Initiation and Coordination of Special Community Events

Too much of what is done in the traditional school has been based on the assumption that if it is worth doing - it is worth a course or formalized program. Educators have too often tended to think in terms of quarters, semesters or neat blocks of time that start and end according to predetermined schedules.

Education II, the community totally mobilized for education, envisions a host of special activities and "happenings" that are scheduled, coordinated and initiated by the community and the school faculty. The programs conducted bring people of all ages together. They tend to establish a new sense of community and the school becomes the social, cultural and educational hub of the community. The special activities have an open admission policy. They are walk-in programs. The schools do not have a captive audience. No registration is required, no attendance is taken and successful programs are repeated. Dr. Frank J. Manley, the founder of the community school programs in Flint, Michigan, once referred to this aspect of community education, as an attempt to make each school "a poor man's country club". The possibilities for programs and activities that serve the interest of a community are so plentiful that no illustrations are necessary.

Component VIII:

The Establishment of Problem Solving Procedures through the Creation of a Citizens Advisory Council

Community education is a process and like most processes is much easier to describe than define. No set of prescriptions will serve all communities. Each school attendance area will be confronted with unique problems. Further, each school attendance area will come up with its own solutions to many of the problems that confront children and adults in their area. These problems cannot be, and in most cases should not be sent to the central office for consideration. Their solution is fostered best when they are given immediate consideration in the local setting, by those directly involved.

Each community school should have a citizens advisory council, a council that serves to inform the school of the community's needs, desires and expectations. In addition, the citizens advisory council assists the professional educators by informing members of the community of problems and goals sensed or expressed from the point of view of educators.

The citizens advisory council, which usually consists of from eight to fifteen people must feel free to bring community schools to the attention of the principal, the community school director and the faculty of the school. In addition, school personnel must develop attitudes that allow them to share decision-making in certain areas with the advisory council. The terms and selection of councils are an individual community decision. However, they should be broadly based consisting of members representing all members of the school community.

It is important to emphasize the advisory nature of the council. A group such as this has *no* administrative authority. This does not lessen the importance of the group. The emphasis is given to the development of creative ideas to be implemented by the Community Director and other members of the administrative staff. Council members, through a process of orientation, become effective participants in the community education process.

Component IX:

The Employment of a Community School Director or Coordinator who Serves to Tie all of the above together and also Serves in the Capacity of an Ombudsman for his Entire Community

What can be done about the rising tendency toward over-centralization, a tendency toward tall, unresponsive bureaucracies, and the proliferation of overlapping agencies that are a result of the fragmentation of efforts directed toward the improvement of lives of individuals and community? It has been stated earlier that individuals and communities are twin-born. The probability for educational success will increase dramatically when a total effort is mobilized toward improving both individuals and the community in which they reside.

The community school director or coordinator serves as a community agent, an agent whose responsibilities lie in bringing all the components of community education together into a working process for individual and community fulfillment and betterment. In his role as a catalytic agent, he brings together the many agencies and services that exist in a community. The community school director also serves in the role of ombudsman, a role not uncommon to many Scandinavian nations. The ombudsman is an information source, a person that knows about services. He is a generalist, a generalist whose specialty is knowledge of existing resources for the betterment of community and individuals that reside within each community. His inservice training consists of keeping abreast of new developments within the community. He remains aware of the educational, social, recreational and cultural opportunities that are available. He operates in much the fashion of the early 1900 ward-healer. However, there is one important distinction here. He does not extract any political price for his services to the community. One of the ironies of our time is the number of children from fatherless homes that need male guidance. (This need may be supplied by service clubs.) As one illustration, the Big Brothers organization strives to find children who have this need and attempts to solve it by providing the people. Too often in our complex society the individual with needs and the service agencies are unaware of each other. The ombudsman, the community director, serves in a role that brings the client and the service agency together. As urbanization increases, and particularly in neighborhoods that are considered disorganized, the role of the ombudsman becomes increasingly important.

Component X:

The Establishment of a Climate for Innovation and Change

Exploratory innovative programs are initiated and explored during the regular school program, after school hours and in summer sessions. American society in general and the educational enterprise is no exception, has become preoccupied with orderly, neat, predictable patterns of change that must result en masse. This notion attempts to improve the total system simultaneously. The acceptance of change and innovation by the central office has created in Education I a tendency toward a feeling of helplessness, dependency and unimaginativeness on parts of faculty at local school levels.

The tendency toward over-centralization has persuaded many citizens, particularly rebellious elements among the young, that innovation, reform or modifications are impossible. In their view, the only recourse is the complete dismantling or destruction of the existing system or establishment.

An important ingredient in the acceptance of the community education philosophy is the acceptance of a flat, horizontal organizational structure. Such a structure provides for unity but allows for diversity among its various sub-systems. Individual schools through community and faculty action are allowed, even encouraged, to innovate, explore and abandon routine. Communities are encouraged to summon their own imaginations, talents and resources to solve local problems, problems that range from lunchroom conduct to drug abuse patterns. In some school districts, local schools are given incentives or innovative grants to use at the local schools discretion. The total community becomes involved in identifying problems, establishing practices and mobilizing and allocating resources toward the solution of identified problems and needs.

Two things are involved in this process. First, problems are identified and individuals, small groups, or the total community can make strides toward their solution. Second, the change process that takes place through the solution of problems is equally important. It is through this process that individuals, groups, communities discover themselves and each other. This point brings us to the next important aspect of community schools, *Heuristics*.

Component XI:

Provisions for Heuristics

The genius of community education is found in the process - a process of doing and becoming. Community education is not a bag of tricks, a gimmick or a package that can be superimposed upon a community. It is a process through which individuals and communities discover themselves and each other. The process provides for discovery and rediscovery. Rediscovery of the joy of learning, the excitement of commitment, the interdependence of individuals and the need for community action.

Each program must therefore be unique. Each program must develop on its own. Each program must reflect the identified wants and the felt needs of its community. The result is a continuous process of self discovery, a sense of individual and community achievement that fosters a positive self concept and pride in "our school" and "our community".

The underlying premise is that doing results in understanding, feelings and attitudes. The heuristic process allows for discovery of new attitudes, new feelings, new understanding and new confidences.

Component XII:

Provisions for Serendipity

Once the philosophy and process of community education has been implemented all sorts of exciting and unpredictable things begin to happen. In the process of implementing one idea, new resources and other ideas emerge. A new excitement is introduced to the educational process. A new optimism in people and community develops.

Community education is an "open system", a receptive concept that searches out fortuitous developments. Every community has untapped talents and unused resources. Education II throws open its doors, welcoming, encouraging and searching for the best in man and community. The results are serendipitous for all individuals and their community.

CONCLUSION

The purpose of community education is to provide its citizens a sense of well-being. What has been lost through urbanization can be regained through the educational programs. With a full utilization of all the resources within the community, the climate for growth is fostered. The greatest need is that of leadership for enlisting the support necessary for change. Citizens must become aware of the goals to be attained and must share in the process for attaining them. This is a process that will take time. If the American dream for education is to become a reality, there is no better avenue for achieving it than that provided by the concept of community education.

CHAPTER XII

WHY EDUCATION II?

WHY EDUCATION II?

A NEW FORM

Community Education is by no means a new idea or novel concept. The concept dates back to the turn of the century. Volumes have been written about community education, the community school, and related subjects.

Many communities have met with outstanding success in even the most superficial acceptance of the concept. Yet the Community Education concept appears to meet with misunderstanding, halfhearted acceptance and in some instances neglect and negative toleration. There is much more here than a hiatus between professional education and the lay public. The paradox of the slow development of a new education is the reluctance of the education establishment to develop new forms, in the face of lay leader demands for more effective, efficient, and relevant educational programs. The destiny of the educational establishment appears to be centered in an inaccessible elite, that has become insensitive to individual protests or opinions. The present educational establishment reacts to community and human concerns with additional fragmented programs. There is a tendency toward capsulating human problems and concerns in neat little packages. Community—School relationships and even the faculties within the school tend to take on qualities that appear to be largely mechanistic. If one examines the flow charts of the established bureaucracy, it is evident that there is little importance given to

181

human concerns, individual consideration, and personal dignity. The irony of it all is that the very institution that has the primary responsibility to develop the individual, has become so insensitive to its clients - that, in effect, it is a major contributor to a pattern that dwarfs the significance of the individual.

Actually the teaching profession has in many cases been the major "road block" to the development of Community Education. Many teachers see a Community School as a mere addition to the usual K-12 program. It may be viewed as a good addition to the "regular" program. It is sometimes seen as a good program to be paid for by special funds. In many established "Community Schools," this inadequate perception prevails. The school is "lighted" and open in the evening. Interesting activities are conducted in the afternoon and evening, but the school for children during the day is untouched by the concept.

Clearly, both the profession and the community need clarification of all educational terminology. The term Community School is inadequate if it is perceived as merely a school which renders services to the community after regular school hours. Even the broader term "Community Education" may be misleading if it is interpreted as the extension of traditional educational forms and practices to a larger audience.

What is needed in American Education today is not a set of additions or band-aids to the existing traditional system, but rather new forms. These new forms pay less attention to product, means, methods and instruments but give more attention to persons, process, ends and ideals.

Humanity II demands a new education. The new education must examine and re-examine existing assumptions. It must set new goals and operate in new dimensions. This will necessitate new roles for lay people, children, teachers, and administrators. Education II must include all that is usually subsumed under the community education "umbrella," but the fragmented prices must have a new relationship. A new horizonal relationship must be developed in which the various parts complement each other.

The **rational** excuse usually given for educational bankruptcy is lack of funds. Lack of money is not the reason we do not have communities that are totally and effectively mobilized for education. If new money becomes suddenly available in amounts adequate to implement a total Community Education program, few new forms would be forthcoming under the present tendency of institutions to react rather than to act. The new money, in all likelihood, would go for more of the same or new fragmented, capsulated, specialized programs that emphasize technological or bureaucratic means rather than ends or new processes.

Compounding the problem is the education professions reverence for a schoolhouse brand of education. Many educators see money spent outside of the schoolhouse for the improvement of the community as money taken away from the education of children. They do not yet perceive the important relationship between - school and community. Nor do they see how inadequate a schoolhouse education can be in a declining, alienated, disaffected community. Many educators still labor under the false assumption that the educational system as it is now constituted can solve American problems if only the public would invest more money in the present system.

The present system of education is a partial, incomplete program that violates what we know about human beings and how they learn and grow. It is the child's total environment that educates. In spite of the fact that there is evidence to support this contention, the educational profession has been indifferent and sometimes hostile to efforts to improve the home and community. The profession has in effect kept parents and the public out of the educational planning endeavor and out of the teaching and learning process. Professional educators tend to insist that education is their province and have jealously kept the public out, or have reluctantly accepted citizens only under carefully controlled terms and conditions.

The public and many educational leaders have become disenchanted with this attitude. Many are beginning to ask why, with our huge and rising costs for schools, do the serious problems persist and continue to magnify? In many metropolitan areas citizens are demanding decentralization and home rule school boards. Some Boards of Education are contracting with the private sector for the education of children. Other school systems are working on various schemes for compensatory education. None of these practices speak to the solution of the real problem. The real problem is that many children do not have a wholesome environment for learning. Therefore, the total environment must receive attention. Patchwork provisions that add a piece here and another there are not the solution to the problem since they have little impact on the total environment.

Education II differs from Education I in that it envisions a process through which all members of a community are given an opportunity to learn, to teach, to contribute and to become involved in the betterment of self, school, and community. Productive assumptions toward this end guide the process. A creative attitude permeates the entire educational climate.

Education I with its stress on detachment, objectivity, and quantifications, has too often failed in the development of attitudes, ethics and values. Education II must bring into focus the importance of humanity. To those committed to objectivity and quantification, consideration such as enthusiasm, love, empathy, and compassion are seen as anti-intellectual. Moreover, Education I has developed into a sorting and selecting institution, rather than a truly educational enterprise. Since it is in the business of selectivity, it has tended to become more elitist in its attitudes toward individuals in the general community. The above analysis is especially true for universities and colleges. If the above trend continues, university teacher preparation programs are designed for producing educators for Education I rather than Education II.

Teacher education for Education II must be involved with the community. It is in the community that one can best acquire the human qualities required for relating successfully with people. Working with people from all walks of life tends to increase one's estimate of human potential. One tends to be less influenced by test scores and formal requirements. Schoolhouse oriented educators are prone to look for only the very bright in verbal areas. But, when one begins to become involved with all segments of the community, it becomes increasingly apparent that the worth of an individual cannot be measured by his verbal or quantitative prowess alone. Human beings have many qualities, characteristics and attributes that shape their destinies and determine their contribution to society. Among them are curiosity, compassion, and persistence in pursuit of a goal.

Education II cannot follow in the steps of Education I and serve as a giant selection and sorting agency for society. On the contrary, it will have as its first goal the marshaling of all human resources within a community, and the development of human potential. It is through this total marshaling of our national and community resources that our nation can mount an education of sufficient power to attack the serious problems of our society with effectiveness. Thus the development of Education II is imperative to the survival of American freedom.

GIVING MEANING AND REALITY
TO THE AMERICAN DREAM

"America", says Eric Hoffer, "is the only new thing in history". We are, in America, a country which is the result of the first authentic revolution.

The result of the revolution was the creation of a country with freedom of thought, freedom of expression, freedom of the press and an opportunity for the people to control their own government. Many revolutions have really been counter-revolutionary in effect. They have exchanged one despotism for another. Often the second autocracy is more thoroughgoing than the one destroyed. Not only to Americans but to people all over the world, there has been something special about America. The word "America" has been seen through the decades of our history as synonymous with freedom. People came here to throw off despotisms at home, others to acquire riches, still others to acquire work but, in short, to fulfill the dream of a better life.

Thomas Wolff wrote, "It is Europeans for the most part who have constructed these great ships but without America they have no meaning. These ships are alive with the supreme ecstasy of the modern world which is the voyage to America. There is no other experience that is remotely comparable to it in its sense of joy, its exultancy, its drunken and magnificent hope which against reason and knowledge soars into a heaven of fabulous conviction which believes in the miracle and sees it invariably achieved."

The central idea of this dream is freedom. Freedom not only from oppression but for a full life, for the development of all one's capacities, for a warm relationship to one's fellowmen, and for participation in ordering the affairs of one's community and one's government. Few among the immigrants who came to our country, or even among our people whose ancestors came in the early years would have expressed it this way, but in America the quest for identity has been more successful to more people than in any other place on earth.

America had its birth in a brilliant vision of human values. The principles of our Declaration of Independence are still new. Some believe they are in advance of the thinking of our people today. Written two hundred years ago, they still state goals for American society and for humanity generally. And a great deal has been accomplished toward realizing the dream. Probably three-fourths of the American people live at a higher economic level than kings could have in the eighteenth and early nineteenth centuries. American education has opened its doors to a larger proportion of the people than would have been thought possible a half century ago, yet our nation is in trouble. It is in trouble because our education has failed to open opportunity to those who need it the most, the poor, the minority groups, the disadvantaged.

As a result we have poverty, unemployment, racial tension, slums, crime, and increasing polarities among our people. Many young people have been losing faith in the American system. Many black people have often convinced themselves there is no hope for integration and have opted for separation. In our large urban areas communication has broken down with a loss of sense of community and personal identity.

To all the malaise of economic and social disadvantage must be added the impact of the war in Southeast Asia, a war increasingly unpopular with the American people and heavily responsible for the current alienation of our young people with their loss of faith in what they call the "establishment". Yet few informed persons would accept the view that if poverty, racial injustice were reduced and the war terminated, a new age of contentment would be with us. The doubts of young and old are too deep, the quandaries too numerous and the conflicts and polarities too sharp. A more plausible view is that we have as a nation begun to question our basic values, even questioning our criteria for truth and value. Consequently, ending war, reducing poverty and eliminating racial prejudice, while they are valid goals for our society, will not in themselves give us a stable, unified, self-repairing society.

There is no thought here of imposing certain values upon our youth and their elders. Rather what is needed is a far more vigorous examination of the American value system, not only by philosophers, teachers and students but an examination carried on jointly by educators, scientists, civic leaders and lay people. Our current educational establishment operated in the way it is does not facilitate such an examination by all concerned.

The result is that the polarities increase and solutions are more and more difficult to achieve. In this volume an effort has been made to suggest an education so different, so intensive, and extended to all the people of the community that we have chosen to use the term Education II.

While elements of such a program are not new, the mobilization and involvement are predicated on a scale that really produces a new education for a new society. As we see Education II it is not an immediate solution for America's problems but it sets in motion a process that will facilitate a self-repairing society.

At present our communities are fragmented by geography, race and economic condition. Our schools and social agencies are so isolated from each other they augment this fragmentation. The process needed is one which sees the entire community with all its resources as an educational enterprise. It visualizes a community which sees education as its major reason for being. Such a community will in the process of its studies sense the inadequacies of our present education and it will realize that an education of new power is required. Fashioning this education may well be the greatest task we in America have ever undertaken. We will not bring this education into being merely by working on the campus and in our schools. The new education will be shaped in American communities and bear the imprint of the work not only of educators but of community people, many of whom were given short-shrift by the present educational establishment. In fact, the very task of developing Education II is an exciting educational undertaking, in which the immediate goal may be the shaping of a new education but with the final outcome of educating lay and professional people to meet the challenges of a constantly changing society.

BIBLIOGRAPHY

Arendt, Hannah. *The Human Condition.* Chicago: The University of Chicago Press, 1958.

Biddle, William W. *The Community Development Process.* New York: Rinehart, Winston, Inc., 1965.

Brownell, Baker. *The Human Community.* New York: Harper & Bros., 1950.

Campbell, Clyde M., *et al. Toward Perfection in Learning.* Midland, Michigan: The Pendell Company, 1969.

Coleman, James. *The Concept of Equal Educational Opportunity.* Harvard Educational Review, 38:1, Winter, 1968.

Coleman, James S., *et al. Equality of Educational Opportunity.* (Washington: U.S. Government Printing Office, 1966), p. 628.

Combs, Arthur S. *The Professional Education of Teachers.* Boston: Allyn & Bacon, Inc., 1965.

Combs, Arthur W., editor. *Perceiving, Behaving, Becoming.* Washington: The National Education Association, 1962.

Conant, James Bryant. *Slums and Suburbs.* New York: McGraw-Hill Book Company, Inc., 1961.

Cremin, Lawrence A. *The Transformation of the School.* New York: Alfred A. Knopf, Inc., 1961.

Davis, Allison. *Social Class Influences Upon Learning.* Cambridge: Harvard University Press, 1948.

Deutsch, Martin. *Happenings on the Way Back to the Forum.* Harvard Educational Review, 39:3, Summer, 1969.

Deutsch and Associates. *The Disadvantaged Child.* New York: Basic Books, 1967.

Drucker, Peter F. *The Age of Discontinuity.* New York: Harper & Row, 1968.

Goldstein, Bernard. *Low Income Youth in Urban Areas.* New York: Holt, Rinehart and Winston, Inc., 1967.

Cordon, Mitchell. *Sick Cities.* New York: The Macmillan Company, 1965.

Green, Robert L. *Racial Crisis in American Education.* Chicago: The Follett Educational Corporation, 1969.

Halpin, Andrew W. and Croft, Don B. *The Organizational Climate of Schools.* Chicago: The University of Chicago.

Harrington, Michael. *The Other America.* New York: The Macmillan Company, 1963.

_____. *Harvard Educational Review.* Vol. 39. Cambridge: Harvard University.

Hickey, Howard W. *The Role of the School in Community Education.* Midland, Michigan: The Pendell Company, 1969.

Hoffer, Eric. *The True Believer.* New York: Harper & Row, Inc., 1951.

Holt, John. *How Children Fail.* New York: Pittman Publishing Corporation, 1964.

Horney, Karen. *Our Inner Conflict.* New York: Morton, 1945.

Hunter, Floyd. *Community Power Structure.* Chapel Hill: The University of North Carolina Press, 1953.

Jencks, Christopher and Riesman, David. *The Academic Revolution.* New York: Doubleday and Company, 1968.

Jensen, Arthur R. *Reducing the Heredity Environment Uncertainty:* A Reply. Harvard Educational Review, 39:3 Summer, 1969.

Jersild, Arthur T. *In Search of Self.* New York: Bureau of Publications, Teachers College, Columbia University.

Kerber, August and Smith, Wilfred R. *Educational Issues in a Changing Society.* Detroit: Wayne State University Press, 1964.

Kohl, Herbert R. *The Open Classroom.* New York: Review - Vintage 116, 1969.

Kozol, J. *Death at an Early Age.* Boston: Houghton Miflin, 1967.

Leonard, George B. *Education and Ecstasy.* New York: Delacorte Press, 1968.

Likert, Rensis. *New Patterns in Management.* New York: McGraw-Hill Book Co. Inc., 1961.

Maslow, Abraham H. *Eupsychian Management.* Homewood, Illinois: Richard D. Irwin Inc. and the Dorsey Press, 1965.

Mayo, Elton. *The Social Problems of an Industrial Civilization.* Boston: Graduate School of Business Administration, Harvard University, 1945.

McGregor, Douglas. *The Human Side of Enterprise.* New York: McGraw-Hill Book Co. Inc., 1960.

Melby, Ernest O. *The Teacher and Learning.* Washington: The Center for Applied Research in Education Inc., 1963.

Miller, David R. and Swanson, Gary E. *Inner Conflict and Defense.* New York: Holt, Rinehart and Winston, 1960.

Moustakas, Clark E. *Loneliness.* New York: Prentice-Hall, Inc., 1961.

National Society for the Study of Education Fifty-Second. *Yearbook.* LII, The Community School, 1953.

Olson, Edward. *The Modern Community School.* New York: Appleton, Century, Crofts, Inc., 1953.

Passow, A. Harry. *Education in Depressed Areas.* New York: Bureau of Publications, Teachers College, Columbia University, 1963.

Pfuetze, Paul E. *The Social Self,* New York: Bookman Associates, 1954.

Postman, Neil and Weingartner, Charles. *Teaching as a Subversive Activity.* New York: Delacorte Press, 1970.

Raubinger, Frederick M. and Rowe, Harold G. *The Individual and Education.* New York: The Macmillan Company, 1968.

Rees, Helen. *Deprivation and Compensation Education.* Boston: Houghton-Miflin Co., 1968.

_____. *Report of the National Advisory Commission on Civil Disorders.* Washington: U.S. Government Printing Office, 1968.

Riessman, Frank. *The Culturally Deprived Child.* New York: Harper, 1962.

Rosenthal, Robert and Jacobson, Lenore. *Pygmalion in Classroom.* New York: Holt, Rinehart and Winston, Inc., 1968.

Sexton, Patricia Cayo. *Education and Income.* New York: The Viking Press, 1964.

Silberman, Charles E. *Crisis in the Classroom.* New York: Random House, 1970.

Silberman, Charles E. *Crisis in Black and White*. New York: Random House Inc., 1964.

Totten, W. Fred and Manley, Frank J. *The Community School*. Galien, Michigan: Allied Education Council, 1969.

Totten, W. Fred. *The Power of Community Education*. Midland: Pendell Publishing Co. 1970.

Vose, Clement. *Affirmative School Integration*. Beverly Hills, California: Sage Publications, 1967.

Whitt, Robert L. *A Handbook for the Community School Director*. Midland, Michigan: Pendell Publishing Co., 1971.

BIBLIOTHÈQUE CHAMPLAIN

3 9365 00156531 8